"Alan Uke provides simple, breakthrough ways to empower the American people to actually impact our trade deficit. Anyone who is a consumer and is concerned with the state of the U.S. economy should read this book. It will make us a better informed society able to chart a secure and prosperous course forward in the world economy."

—**Carlos Gutierrez**, Former U.S. Secretary of Commerce and former Chief Executive Officer, Kellogg Company

"The public   he country,
for workers   this simple
point: Work   should be
empowered   nds should
be part of a   g strategy."

                                                          ent AFL-CIO

"*Buying Am*   erested in
stimulating   e products
are produce   anymore.
Alan clearly   a product
is made an   States. By
educating c   choice and
economic fr   rams have
failed—mov

                                                          ray (R-CA)

"There is a   ying products in Americ   couraging
economic grow   he cutting
edge of that mov   sumer culture to appreciate   ts. Amen,
and it's about time   cts."

—**Jerry Jasinowski**   ufacturers

"Alan Uke serves America well, by giving our citizens the information they need to buy products that reflect not only good value, but American jobs as well."

—Ret. U.S. Rep. **Duncan Hunter**, Former Chairman of the House Armed Services Committee

BUYING
AMERICA
BACK

A Real-Deal Blueprint for Restoring American Prosperity

ALAN UKE

SelectBooks, Inc.
New York

Copyright © 2012 by Alan Uke

This edition published by SelectBooks, Inc.
For information address SelectBooks, Inc., New York, New York.

First Edition

ISBN 978-1-59079-230-8

Cataloging-in-Publication Data
Uke, Alan.
  Buying America back : a real-deal blueprint for restoring American prosperity / Alan Uke. – 1st ed.
      p. cm.
  Includes bibliographical references.
  Summary: "A successful American entrepreneur offers solutions to the loss of American jobs and manufacturing. To help consumers understand buying choices, he advocates a movement to pass laws to label imports with the percentages of a product's costs of manufacture in the countries of origin and data showing whether trade ratios are balanced and beneficial to the United States"–Provided by publisher.
  ISBN 978-1-59079-230-8 (pbk. : alk. paper)
1. United States–Economic policy–2009- 2. Competition–United States.
3. Price regulation–United States. 4. Consumer goods–Labeling. 5.
Consumer behavior–United States. I. Title.
  HC106.84.U35 2012
  338.973–dc23
                              2011044130

Interior book design by Janice Benight

Manufactured in the United States of America
10 9 8 7 6 5 4 3 2 1

*This book is dedicated to the workers displaced,
the factories closed, the small towns decimated, and
the opportunities denied to the people of America. It is
also dedicated to all of us, the consumers, whose money
has been harvested by those who work against us.*

CONTENTS

PART ☆ ONE
Buying America Back   1

PART ☆ TWO
Consumer Travelogue   83

ACKNOWLEDGMENTS

This book began at the dinner table. I was complaining about the state of things and expressing ideas about "why don't they do this and this." As I remember, it was my daughter Leslie who infamously said to me, "Dad, so why don't you write a book?" I looked around the table at my engineer-daughter, my majored-in-English-in-college step-daughter, and my majored-in-linguistics-in-college son-in-law, and thoughts began to come: . . . I have ideas, but not the time or aptitude to write a good book, but . . . if I could conscript these people . . . it might happen.

I thank my son-in-law Arto Jaakkola for doing most of the research and first-draft writing; I want to thank my step-daughter Lauren Wilkinson for editing and crafting the book into something that was accessible and easy to read, and I want to thank my daughter Leslie Uke for her ideas and preparation of the illustrations and graphs used in the book.

I also want to thank my wife Amie and my sons Greg and John for their continuing support and editorial comments.

I have the good fortune to have Bill Gladstone as my agent, who used his talents and connections to both find us a publisher and negotiate a fair contract; Barbara Villasenor and Myra Westphall of First Reads, who did the first professional editing and added a great deal of energy and ideas; Kenzi Sugihara, the publisher and Nancy Sugihara, the editor at SelectBooks, who courageously tackled the work of editing and turning my manuscript into a book; and finally, Meryl Moss of Meryl L. Moss Media Relations, who took on the enormous task of the publicity and marketing of the book.

LETTER TO MY SON

Dear John,

I am writing this letter to you to make you aware, if you are not already, that your future—our future—could become very bleak if we don't take action. I want to offer your generation, and all of us, a hopeful and practical solution. That solution is the most important reason I have written this book.

Things have changed dramatically since I was a young man like you, ready to set off into the world. I had many opportunities to explore. The road ahead looked bright. When I think of the rough road you now have to face, I am heartbroken. So many jobs have disappeared. Even someone as creative and hardworking as you will face major obstacles to finding stable and fulfilling employment.

I will personally do whatever it takes to make change possible. I have started with this book: I have written it not only to explain how we've got into this monumental mess, but to give you, give all Americans, a solution for how we can significantly turn this situation around in just a few years.

With confidence and hope,
Dad

INTRODUCTION

Wherever you are, pause for a moment. Look at the objects around you. Perhaps you are lucky enough to be reading this outdoors where much of what surrounds you is created by nature. Look at what you have with you and what you are wearing. If you are indoors, look at the things you use every day. Chances are, wherever you are reading this book, you are surrounded by many, many objects that are man-made and produced in factories by people and machines.

Before you read on, pick up five of the objects and look at them more closely. You rely on many of these things. Ask yourself this: Where do they come from?

Look for the country of origin label.

Very likely, most of what you found was not made in the U.S.A.

And there may have been some surprises. If you were in the kitchen you might have noticed that almost anything with an electric cord on it, no matter how familiar the American brand, was made in China.

There is also much that the label doesn't tell you. In all likelihood, many of the objects have components from all over. You weren't told the whole story when you made your purchase. Something doesn't feel right, does it?

You use many of these objects on a daily basis. They are supposed to bring you comfort and well-being and yet their country of origin label hints at a deeper, more disturbing truth.

Why is it important to know where the things we buy are made? For starters, the country that makes the product you buy gets the money you spend. Years ago, most things we bought were made in American factories by American workers. The money stayed here in the U.S. and was used to build factories and create jobs. Today, 60% of the manufactured consumer goods we buy are imported from other countries.[1] This means 60% of the money you spend for these goods is sent out of the United States, keeping people and companies in other countries employed and making money. Meanwhile our job base is disappearing, deficits are ballooning and our future looks bleak.

Consider the objects you found once again. Even though they may deliver moments of satisfaction or comfort, in many cases their very purchase quietly undermines your future economic stability, slowly erodes your standard of living, and chips away at the economic foundation you worked hard to build. All the while, another country is reaping the benefits of all that we lose.

The economic foundation of our country has been severely eroded over the past forty years. I am not talking only about the millions of factory jobs that have been lost, but also the creative people in research and development, and our professionals—such as engineers, scientists, and chemists—who are being replaced by outsourcing. Our future as a nation and as individuals is being threatened.

Since our spending habits as consumers have contributed to this situation, we can change our spending habits to reverse it. If we don't, we are all in for tougher times.

In order to make this change we need more information at the point of sale about where the product is made that includes where the manufacturer is located and where the manufacturer spent money to produce it. In many cases more than one country is involved in the process, and we need labels that give complete information about the countries of origin of the product so we can be better informed when we choose which products we want to buy.

It is not enough to be angry and frustrated about our economy. In order for a change to happen, consumers must demand to be more honestly and completely informed about what they are buying and where their money goes. To this end, we are starting a *consumer movement* to bring this to the attention of Congress. We want them to enact laws for more thorough labeling, just like the government responded to the demand that the food industry reveal precise content information on every packaged food product. The goal of this movement and of this book is to encourage people to change their buying habits toward purchasing things that help the U.S. economy and job situation.

You are not alone. We have to band together before it's too late. The American people are the largest block of consumers on the planet! We have immense power. Consumer spending makes up seventy percent of the U.S. economy.[2] This means that we, taking determined action together, have an enormous influence on what happens to us in the future—by directly and indirectly revitalizing America's manufacturing and job base.

We have the same situation about this consumer issue that we had with unsafe cars, unwholesome food, unsafe use of insecticides, and damage to our environment. Many corporations want us to believe that when they prosper, America prospers. That's rarely true. Business interests are not in alignment with the American people's economic interests. Our government is unable to act because it's pandering to business interests that conflict with what is best for the consumer. Only a populist movement that refuses to buy products that are not beneficial to the American people can move business to act differently. Only a populist movement that refuses to vote for candidates who do not advocate America's best interests can move politicians to act differently.

Many of us are not as well off as we might have been twenty or thirty years ago. But you do not need to be rich to make change. Changing our spending habits even slightly will have a massive effect on our economy and our own lives. Later in this book, I discuss how other countries do just that, and have built successful economies with similar measures. We need to create our own consumer movement along these lines, or face the consequences.

This book explains why this is important and why it will work. Other countries are thriving, enjoying a high wage and a high standard of living. We can once again have this, too, but only by taking action together now. When you have the tools to make thoughtful buying decisions and can purchase wisely, you not only invest in your own well-being, but in the prosperity of America.

PART ★ ONE

Buying America Back

☆ Chapter 1 ☆

THE WAY FORWARD

Would you believe me if I told you we have the power to start putting our economy on its feet again in one year? I'm talking about creating more jobs in our country, enjoying products that are better-made, putting more cash into the pockets of our citizens, eliminating our trade deficit, and significantly reducing our national debt. This may seem like a tall order but it's doable and realistic.

The primary purpose of this book is to start an essential consumer movement—a movement that will stimulate a new way of thinking about what you buy. I want to focus on what happens to the money we spend. Where does it go? Who gets it? What kinds of consequences do our everyday purchases have in the world? What are the consequences to our personal future employment and wages, or even the long-standing security of our country and its citizens? To approach these questions, I mainly discuss the U.S. economy, because it is vital to us and affects all of our lives on a daily basis. Ours is still the world's largest economy by a huge margin. That means we have immense power as consumers. We keep the gears of this country, and those of the world, moving.

We also import more goods than anyone else.[1] Our purchases have far-reaching effects in the world. Every dollar you spend has an effect. For example, if we buy clothes from a company that makes them in a degrading sweatshop in Nepal, we are participating in that abuse. On the other hand, if we buy from a company in Costa Rica that is actively conserving the environment, we are participating in the fight to save Earth's resources.

How do your purchases affect these issues? Think about it. Your money goes to a factory that contributes to global warming or to air pollution, and that extra demand causes them to expand and pollute more. It is the direct result of your spending. Your spending influences the world. It creates jobs,

3

it affects who gets paid and where. Your spending affects the environment, human rights, the development of geographic and industrial areas, and even the economics of entire nations.

Since we are the largest-consuming nation on the planet and live with a sense of abundance, how did it happen that there are fewer jobs and we are getting poorer? Several decades ago America was the epicenter of thriving manufacturing and service industries. Today, a great many of our factories are deserted, stable jobs have disappeared, and the working middle class is steadily shrinking. Where did it all go wrong? What happened to American jobs?

The answer is quickly revealed by checking the tags on most of the items in your closet. Where were they made? Walk into any supermarket and fill a cart with an assortment of everyday items. Scan the packaging and look for the tiny print "Made in . . ." What follows this text? If you perform this simple task, more than likely you will see that most of these items have not been made in America. What was once our booming, innovative manufacturing industry has been exported overseas and with it, an alarming number of American jobs.

The same is now true even of our service industries. Having trouble with a product you purchased from an American company? When you call the help-line, chances are your call will be routed abroad.

The simple answer is that to bring back American jobs and support the American economy, we must change our buying habits and purchase products that are manufactured here, or at least purchase products from foreign countries that have balanced trade alliances with the U.S. But going about this seemingly simple endeavor is not as easy as it sounds.

Ironically, in the "Age of Information," Americans have little access to clear, truthful representations of a product's origins. Typically, components of a product can be manufactured in any number of countries. "Made in America" does not necessarily mean "Made in America." What that product sticker or seal may not disclose is that although it was assembled in America, its components were made elsewhere by foreign workers, to the advantage of someone else's economy.

After 9/11 President George W. Bush advised Americans to support and prop up our economy by going shopping. He said the same thing as a recession was looming in 2007.[2] Consumption drives our economy. Unfortunately, because such a huge share of what we buy is imported, our shopping sprees often support not our own economy, but the economies of foreign countries. When we go shopping out of a patriotic duty, as President Bush encouraged us all to do, we are in fact sending a vast majority of that money overseas for the benefit of other nations and simultaneously expanding our current account deficit. And we don't necessarily know this because what we call "country of origin labeling" is so deficient. Understanding the origins of a product's manufacturing can be an essential tool enabling us to take back control of the consumer-spending engine of our economy. It's like driving a car; once you have a windshield you can clearly see through, you can drive where you want to go.

In order to support our economy and American industries we must have easily accessible, clearly communicated, and truthful information about a product's entire origins. What follows in this book advocates marking goods with the percentage and origin of content as well as the nationality and location of the manufacturer. Our purchasing choices are remarkably powerful and perhaps our only hope to influence the re-location of jobs to our country as well as actions of governments and companies to encourage this.

Personally, I want to know where my goods come from so I can make an informed choice. I am not an isolationist, or even really a protectionist. Even if every other country in the world were to openly practice protectionist policies while we wave our jobs goodbye in the spirit of free trade, I do not wish to shut our country out of world trade. Wouldn't that be short-sighted and foolish? Trade is very good for this country. But it is only good when it is balanced.

We have been programmed to demand cheaper goods. Companies have lured us in with the enticement of saving money. But, by buying something cheaper, we have cost ourselves more in the long run. We think we are saving money, but we are losing it in the bigger picture. Our demand for "cheap" gives fuel to American businesses to manufacture elsewhere.

It is going to require changing our habits and recommitting ourselves to supporting American businesses to solve our trade imbalance. We have to make it a national priority to bring the manufacturing of products back to our country and to encourage companies that currently have their offices and factories in America to stay here.

This is not easy, but it *is* possible. Changing our economy necessitates changing our culture—undoing years of careless habits that have become the norm. I hope what I share will empower you to engage in a new movement of voter and consumer action. Our greatest power lies in how we spend our money and how we vote. Knowing that, the only real value of a solution is when it is followed by consistent, forward-moving action.

It's my goal to have this book open a new kind of discussion and thoughtfulness about where your money goes. We hear a lot about all the bad things threatening us in the future, and it often seems so beyond our control that it can be discouraging to do anything about them. You have real power right now. Every dollar in your wallet and how you spend it effects change. You cast a ballot for the kind of future you want with every purchase. I strongly believe that you deserve to know exactly what you are voting for.

THE U.S. ECONOMY IN A NUTSHELL

Want our closed factories re-opened? Want to bring big cities and small towns back to life?

We have a GDP (Gross Domestic Product, in other words, everything we produce) of around 15 trillion dollars. When we say 70% of the economy is consumer spending, it is because around 10 trillion dollars of it is spent by individuals. There are about 330 million Americans, and the average person has around 30 thousand dollars of it going through their hands each year. That's around 100 dollars a day for every man, woman, and child.

When we put labels on products to encourage purchases which are beneficial to the United States, we can begin to change our buying habits. If each person shifted just one percent ($1 per day) of their spending, we would see instant change. By each person spending just one dollar more per day on products manufactured in America, we would shed 100 billion dollars from the trade deficit. If each billion dollar shift in the trade deficit translates to 13,000 jobs, this would create 1.3 million jobs in America. More than the stimulus package produced—with just one dollar per person each day!

If we made a concerted effort, like the Germans, to reduce our trade deficit by shifting our spending 10% or 10 dollars a day, we would create 13 million jobs. We would solve our unemployment problem; in fact, more people would have to join the workforce. Instead of people competing for jobs, companies would be competing for employees. Wages, benefits, and working conditions would improve by the competition for workers. That is why German factory workers get paid 12 dollars an hour more than most American factory workers. People would have jobs, which would give them more than unemployment checks do, wages would rise, and others would elect to join the workforce. Many people would be lifted out of poverty and our all-important middle class would be restored to prosperity.

☆ Chapter 2 ☆

A BUSINESS OWNER'S PERSPECTIVE

I own a company that manufactures consumer and industrial goods. It's not a huge company, but it employs over a hundred people and it's been located in California for forty-one years now. Although we don't get the press that major public companies do, the small and mid-sized businesses (5000 employees and less) make up the majority of the U.S. economy and provide over half of all jobs in the country.[1] Through my business I've made a lot of close friends who own huge companies—incredibly wealthy people. Few of my friends make anything in America anymore. Why is that? One of them once said to me, "America is done." It might not sound patriotic—and it isn't—but what he means is he doesn't believe there is money to be made in America any more. Most of my peers have given up and moved along to lower-wage nations, mostly in Asia, where much higher profits can be made.

I'm not even close to accepting that "America is done." I could quickly make much greater profits by moving production to China where labor is cheaper, but I have stayed put in California where I started my company in 1971. I have made a commitment to keep my operations in America and create jobs for other Americans. I'm far from ready to give up.

Yes, America has lost a whole lot of factories; we have lost many jobs. Though we still make a lot of things here, compared to forty years ago we have lost a huge share of that pie. What's more, we now consume a lot more foreign goods and many of our companies have foreign ownership. But the business leaders who could afford to make things here choose not to. Profits are greater elsewhere.

To be accurate I must admit that my products are not 100% American, sad to say. Certain components I am forced to outsource abroad, mostly to Asia. Sometimes American suppliers are unavailable or would make our products too expensive to be competitive. But we have only one plant, and it's in California. It's where I have lived most of my life and it's where I would like to keep my business. Keeping Americans working is important to me and, logically, should be important to you. But soon enough, if nothing changes and we continue on this path, I will possibly have to join the thousands of other companies who have been forced to either close their doors, or move their production offshore.

In the thirty-five years that my company has dealt in international trade, we have expanded our sales to over sixty countries. If you want to see what the stamps on my passport are, look at our international dealer list: we are one of the few remaining American companies that exports over half of our products. I have traveled overseas over one hundred times, with many trips to China, Taiwan, South Korea, and Japan. I have personally dealt for decades with issues that are hurting our economy, and along the way have formulated a plan on how to repair ours.

Something must be done. We need to create a powerful *advantage* for manufacturers to make things in America.

My History

For as long as I can remember, I have always had a fascination about the way things worked. As a child, it was not unusual for me to pull apart a gadget to understand how it did what it did, and to put it back together in a way that made it work more efficiently. I admired innovators and leaders who thought outside the box—my idols were Henry Ford and Jacques Cousteau. It was no surprise when I ended up studying engineering at the University of California at San Diego and later started a company manufacturing scuba diving equipment out of my dorm room.

As I've mentioned, I live in San Diego and manufacture my products here. All of this has a price, though. Not only is the cost of living high; it has always been made incredibly difficult to operate a manufacturing company here by local, state, and federal governments that don't value manufacturing. Meanwhile, in the forty-plus years since I have been in business, some of my American competitors have moved their production to Asia and are now able to provide lower-cost products with significantly lower capital investment. A few of my foreign competitors have received huge grants from their governments to build tooling and buy machinery elsewhere. They can also introduce products more quickly, having an inexhaustible source of willing labor overseas. Their profits are higher because they don't price their products proportionately lower with their costs. They can then use these extra margins to offer retailers higher margins than domestic products. They can also do more marketing, research and development (R & D), and have more capital to make new products. My company, Underwater Kinetics, has had to rely on being exceptional at innovating and engineering products, obsessive about efficiency, and having a small niche in order to survive.

The truth is, despite the challenges and the heartache, I like making my products in the U.S. because I want to help our country. Americans take pride in making high-quality, remarkably-engineered products that are designed to last for decades. There is truth in the generalization that almost everything is better-made in the U.S. It's because the people making the goods actually use them, understand the product's purpose, and care about what it is they are making

Many imported products, especially those that meet the demand to be produced cheaply, are made by businesses that are in it solely to make money. The longevity of a product is seldom a consideration. These companies don't take the time to educate their overseas employees, so the people creating the consumer goods that have flooded our markets usually don't have a clue about what the item does or how it is used. They have no understanding of the item's poor value or even lack of safety for the user who might be endangered as well as inconvenienced by the inferior performance and premature failure of a product.

It is too late for pointing fingers at persons to blame. The current mess belongs to all of us, and we are all responsible for how we got here, just as we are all needed to repair the damage. It's as though we have spent the past thirty years aboard a cruise ship gorging ourselves on a buffet of endless delights, and now we are so grossly obese that our combined weight is sinking the ship. You can actually *feel* it, can't you?

If one person repents, refusing to gorge on the buffet, the ship will not be saved. In order to save our sinking economy, it will require the sum total of everyone's efforts. This means we must collectively change our attitudes

toward consumption of foreign goods, opting instead for domestically manufactured products or those made by countries that have balanced trade with
our own. This is critical to the health of the national "economic diet"—if a
change is not made, our cruise ship will be on the ocean floor.

Whether we make a change or not I, as a business owner, will actually
be okay. I love making my products in America, but if it becomes unprofit-
able to continue to do so, or impossible because I can no longer buy enough
parts here, I can move my operations overseas like many other business
owners have done. Why am I writing this book, then, if it doesn't outright
serve me and I am not in a place where my business survival is threatened? One reason is that I spent my early youth with my father doing
archeology in Southern Mexico, and when my family moved back to Los
Angeles I was actually ridiculed in front of the class by my teacher and
peers for my accent and poor English. That moment is burned into my
memory, and I've had a ceaseless empathy for the underdog since that
day. Really, it is not the business owners who are suffering; it's the American workers, the new underdogs in the world economy, who are in peril.
They are in the minority of people of the modern world for whom things are
getting worse.

Perhaps I am like the protagonist of *The Insider*, propelled by a combination of conscience and stupidity, in the sense of working against my own
business interest. (The movie featured a tobacco company executive who
came out as a whistleblower against his own company's actions.) I want to
see the American worker regain security and prosperity. I not only want to
keep my factory here in America; I want to see more companies return,
bringing jobs back with them. I want us to stop undermining the society of
our children and grandchildren.

As it stands, we have not only exported our jobs. The jobs that have
disappeared were higher-paying manufacturing jobs, a double whammy to
the American workforce, many of whom are now either unemployed or
forced to accept lower-paying jobs in the service industry. *U.S. factories
lost 5.2 million jobs from 2000 to 2010.* These are unlikely to come back
unless there is a surge in demand (here or abroad) for our products.[2] The
dip in U.S. manufacturing jobs is accompanied by a swell in jobs created
abroad: the 2.9 million U.S. jobs cut by large, multinational corporations
over the past decade went to sub-contractors and 2.4 million workers hired
at their overseas operations.[3]

MY LABELING EXPERIENCE

Ironically, I am one of the few Americans with actual experience about what needs to be done. Years ago, while I was Vice Chairman of our local Boy Scout Council, regulators started implementing a program mandating all companies that employ fifty or more people to enforce a ride-sharing program for their employees. I didn't want this pushed on my people, and I knew the effect it would have on the Cub Scout program. Mothers wouldn't be able to take their kids to den meetings.

As an engineer and manufacturer, I knew that such a program would have a marginal effect on air pollution. The real culprit was the cars themselves. Some cars still legally registered on the road produce a hundred times the pollution of modern ones. Even current models varied two to three times in the amount of the pollution they created.

What I thought might work was to create a "Smog Index" for cars which would tell consumers how much their specific model polluted. This would educate those who cared about air pollution, and would allow these people to choose a less polluting car. California laws allowed me to "sponsor" a bill, which State Senator Robert Presley carried, to implement this change in lieu of mandatory ride sharing. After two years of dealing with everyone from the EPA and car manufacturers to the Sierra Club and car collectors, the bill passed. My "Smog Index" eventually ended up on all cars sold in the U.S.

Interestingly, when I had a meeting with the Engineering Managers of GM, Ford, and Chrysler, I found that the U.S. car manufacturers actually wanted to make lower polluting cars. They breathe our air. Market forces pushed them toward making cars with maximum horsepower and amenities. Once the lower pollution could be touted as a good concept, they actively lobbied for my idea.

The large, multinational corporations and politicians they support have little incentive for fixing these problems, especially as the present situation generously lines their pockets. They want to keep the status quo and they will not relinquish their old ways easily. As depressing as that realization may be, this sinking ship still can be saved. It must start with the American consumer—the vital piece upon which the entire economy relies, because our purchasing decisions can make a great difference in the economy.

It is urgent for you to see why purchasing choices are so important and to understand how other countries' governments and citizens, in contrast to ours, made themselves prosperous by their choice to give preference to their domestically-made products. It is important to understand how many large corporations deceptively keep you uninformed and misinformed about where the money you spend actually goes. Most importantly, this book provides a simple solution that will serve as a tool for us to take control and change the course of our economic future.

Chapter 3

THE IMPORTANCE OF MANUFACTURING FOR AMERICA

"When we buy manufactured goods, we get the goods and the foreigner gets the money. When we buy the manufactured goods at home, we get both the goods and the money."

—ABRAHAM LINCOLN

From a Speech on the Tariff

Much of the story of America's success is written in our history of manufacturing innovation. While revolutionizing the way things were made with quality, efficiency, and astounding speed, we also effectively employed our population. The equation is simple: steady employment instigates and enables spending; spending bolsters the economy—but *only* if a proportion of that money stays in our country.

A potent and revolutionary example is the automobile. Henry Ford led the way in Detroit in the early part of the 20th century by introducing a system for mass production that made the car affordable to many. America became the flagship of personal transportation. With superior production methods and strong investment the American manufacturers garnered a huge slice of the automobile market from the get-go. It took over a half a century before the American car manufacturers were wrestled aside by the foreign companies from Europe and Japan that were aggressively playing catch-up while the American "Big Three"—Ford, General Motors, and Chrysler—had become complacent and overly confident in their leadership position. That attitude is mirrored in the makeup of our entire economy today.

In recent years a staggering increase in the quantity of products we import to the United States has suffocated our domestic manufacturing industry. As an example, in 1960, 8% of the manufactured consumer

TRADE IS LIKE A JAR OF MARBLES

Why is trade good? My favorite way of explaining it is by use of a simple analogy:

We, as a nation, share a large jar of marbles that we use to trade with. As individuals we exchange goods or services for marbles from the jar. When we buy something within the country, the marbles we use as payments stay in the jar. The marbles in this way are circulating, but the amount of marbles in our jar does not change.

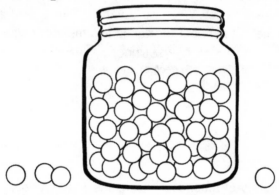

When we engage in trade with a foreign nation (or a company in a foreign nation) we take out marbles to pay for what we are buying. If we have balanced trade with that country, they also buy something from us and give us back the same number of marbles, keeping our marble jar full.

This is a great scenario. It works out for both parties. We can even help out small countries by giving them a few marbles, hoping that they will someday have enough extra marbles to buy from us.

We run into problems when this consistently does not happen—when we engage in a lot of unbalanced trade. We give our marbles to other countries for products, but they do not buy enough of our product to give us a lot of marbles back. Our jar begins to empty.

We then manufacture less and lose the economies of scale achieved in manufacturing on a larger scale. This reduces our competitiveness with other nations, and this means the price of goods for ourselves rises as well.

Trade is good for us, but only if it is monitored to make sure our marble jar stays full and we are having balanced and healthy trade.

Our trade ratio with each country (see table in part two of this book) shows whether the marble jar is getting more full or becoming empty when trading with that country. 1.0 is an equal trade balance. This means they put as many marbles in our jar as we take out to give them. If a country has a 0.5 trade ratio with us it means for every two marbles we give them they give us only one. A trade ratio of .25 means that we give them four marbles and get only one back. Too many transactions like this will eventually lead to an empty jar.

products Americans purchased were imported. Today, that number has grown to an astonishing 60%! Yet, forty years ago, when imports were less prevalent here and our country was a world leader in manufacturing, we had the world's highest standard of living. We no longer do. In just four short decades since then our buying power has stagnated and the working middle class is barely treading water. For the bottom 90% of earners the average pay has grown just a few hundred dollars since 1980, while costs of essential services like health care have climbed every year. In the thirty year period before that, the average income for the same group grew by over $13,000 when adjusted for inflation. The economy has continued to grow since then, but the money is only going to the top 10% of earners. The rest of Americans are left struggling to pay our bills.[1]

The argument that we need imports to raise our standard of living loses credibility in the face of this fact. In reality, as imports have increased, employment opportunities for our all-important middle class have decreased and the job infrastructure has suffered. Trade deficits show a net displacement of American jobs. So, have you really saved more and are you better-off because you bought cheaper imported goods? I contend that had we not outsourced all these jobs, the lower unemployment rate here and the higher wages paid to our manufacturing workers would have raised middle class income. Some things would cost more, but we would also have more money to pay for them.

U.S. Imports and Exports 2010

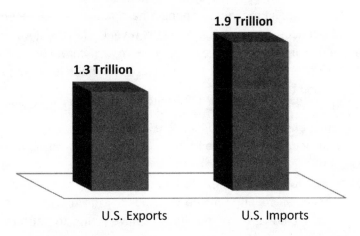

1.9 Trillion

1.3 Trillion

U.S. Exports   U.S. Imports

Source: United States Census Bureau's foreign trade statistics 2010

It is interesting to note that in 1968 there were sixty-two lobbyists in Washington. Lobbyists are usually hired by business and special interest groups. Today, there are 34,000. They outnumber members of Congress *and* their staffers by more than 2 to 1.[2] I believe that the voice and interests of the American people are being drowned out.

As cheap imports have freely flowed in, our own manufacturing base has dwindled. Factories have closed and whole industries have jumped ship and moved abroad. We are falling alarmingly behind in new and modern industries as well, allowing foreign competitors to take over markets that could be very profitable for us for years to come.

Manufacturing jobs are crucial to our local economies and our country as a whole. It is estimated that one manufacturing job creates four or five indirect jobs elsewhere in the economy. In some industries, this number is even higher. One job in automobile production creates 8.6 indirect jobs, in steel manufacturing one job creates 10.3 indirect jobs, and in computer manufacturing it creates 5.6 indirect jobs.[3] For example, car production relies on the rubber industry for tire production, auto supply companies for replacement parts, service company employees for repairs, engineers for the designs, and administrative and marketing staff at the company headquarters for the sales.

If we allow our manufacturing sector to continue to fall away, as is the current trend, the entire economy will suffer unprecedented disaster, and we will all have to settle for a far lower standard of living with staggering unemployment and little hope for the future. Because jobs in manufacturing pay an average of 20% above the pay of jobs in other sectors,[4] the loss of jobs like these means that people have less money to spend on goods and services, and there is less tax revenue for the government to invest in new innovation, education, and infrastructure. For the future health of our economy we need to have and keep these jobs and, more importantly, add to them.

Every product we buy affects our economy. As it stands now, ever-increasing numbers of those products are imported from other countries. As the world became smaller and more integrated as we approached the 21st century, this was to be expected. But the United States' share of imports in relation to its exports has grown more than that of other countries. This has resulted in the U.S. building up bigger and bigger trade deficits, including trade deficits that have grown to astronomical dimensions with just one country: China.[5] This means that we are importing a lot more than we are exporting at this time. *In other words, the trade deficit means that we are consuming more than we are producing.* Commercial ships brimming with Chinese goods are arriving at American docks and leaving empty. Their goods replace all those that we used to manufacture here. In turn, we trade American jobs to China so they can make the goods, practically wishing them bon voyage as they are waved off at the shore. The Economic Policy Institute states this simply in a study examining the effect of America's trade deficit with China: "While it is true that exports support jobs in the United States, it is equally true that imports displace them."[6] This is reflected in the nation's trade balance—for years now deep in red.

Currently, our imports are 17% of the gross domestic product (GDP) while our entire manufacturing sector makes up only 11.5%. Economist Ian Fletcher points out this statistic means "We could quite literally export our entire manufacturing output and *still* not balance our trade."[7] This is a precarious position. America's *trade ratio,* the ratio between imports and exports, is one of the least balanced in the world at 1.24 to 1. This means that we are importing almost 25% more than we are exporting. The ideal trade ratio would be 1 to 1. Our culture of mindless consumption has sent us into a downward spiral. Analogies to overeating work well in describing our situation: we are obliviously, voraciously consuming foreign products to the point of becoming immobile and powerless. Is it any wonder we are also the fattest nation in the world?

The country's economy is in bad shape—that immobility and lack of power is the reality we face. Almost every state in the union is facing budget deficits at the time of this writing. And, of course, the federal deficit is ballooning, almost insurmountably, requiring seemingly endless borrowing just to fund the country's continued operation.[8] The troubled economy includes the massive, record-breaking trade deficits that our nation has amassed in the last decade with consistently rising shortfalls in our exports. Does this make any sense whatsoever? In understanding how best to deliver ourselves from this mess, we must have the honesty and courage to look in the mirror and candidly face the decisions and events that put us where we are, and then do something about it.

In 1971 a trade deficit of just one tenth of today's deficit scared the Nixon administration into approving a series of protectionist measures.

Today, a constantly ballooning deficit is being defended by free trade advocates as something that will simply correct itself in the long run. It won't, and the sooner we react, the better.

We now regularly report trade deficits of hundreds of billions of dollars. In 2010, this number was $633 billion, down from the record of over $800 billion from 2008, "thanks" to the global recession that had a huge negative impact on purchasing power in the United States. Prior to the year 2000, that number had never been over $300 billion. But the number continues to rise. Year-to-year comparison shows that the January 2011 trade deficit was 30% higher than it was in January of 2010. Yet again, the country is on track for another astronomical trade deficit in 2011.[9] The decline of manufacturing in America is directly responsible for this. Since we are manufacturing fewer things, more things need to be imported to cover our own needs.

Take America's current trade deficit with China, which in 2010 reached $260 billion. The Department of Commerce under both President George H. W. Bush and President Clinton estimated that each $1 billion in a trade deficit translates to about 13,000 lost jobs right here in our country.[10] I think we can all agree that we cannot afford to lose any more jobs.

A *Wall Street Journal* article from September 2011, citing an independent MIT study, confirmed what we should already know: areas that lost manufacturing jobs to cheap imports and outsourcing also suffered job losses in other sectors as well, creating depressed wages across all sectors. As people lose their jobs the government has to pick up the tab for unemployment payments, government sponsored health care, and other costs. With government costs soaring and people losing their jobs, the benefits of being able to buy cheaper imported goods disappear completely.[11]

Complacency and lack of investment in essential infrastructure are two factors in the demise of the economy. Companies seeking higher profits have outsourced their production to low-wage countries at the expense of the American worker. Big box retailers looking to sell the products on their shelves for cheaper and cheaper prices have made the problem worse by encouraging—even pressuring—American companies to ship their manufacturing facilities abroad.

The biggest red flag concerning this rearrangement of labor and deficits is not the outsourcing of traditional high-labor industries like apparel and small household goods to low-wage countries, but the gradual

2010 Imports from China by Category

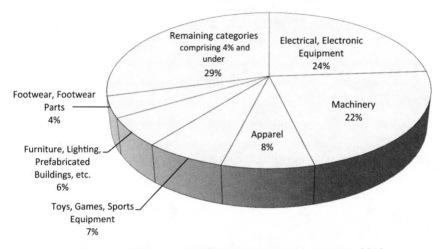

Remaining categories comprising 4% and under
29%

Electrical, Electronic Equipment
24%

Footwear, Footwear Parts
4%

Machinery
22%

Furniture, Lighting, Prefabricated Buildings, etc.
6%

Apparel
8%

Toys, Games, Sports Equipment
7%

Source: United States Census Bureau's foreign trade statistics 2010

disappearance of American high-tech innovation in favor of high-quality imports. Astoundingly, even though we invented and originally manufactured the computer here, we have currently outsourced that production to such an enormous extent that China's number one export to the United States is computer equipment—to the tune of $46 billion a year! You would be hard-pressed to find a computer that is made in the United States anymore. One of our largest deficits is in high-technology goods, an industry we could stand to gain a lot from by producing them here again. Instead, America's top export to China is waste paper and scrap metal, totaling $8 billion in 2010.[12]

As we approached the 21st century, there was an assumption that America would be shifting from low-tech industries to high-tech industries. It hasn't happened. There are absolutely no new jobs being generated in manufacturing. Zero. Over five million manufacturing jobs have vanished from 2001 to 2011. These jobs are not coming back. Only 11 million people now work in manufacturing in the United States, a historical low. The last time America employed fewer people in manufacturing was in 1941[13] —when the population was 133 million. (Today the U.S. population is about 311 million.) This change is striking.

It is not simply the industries of the past and high-tech ventures that are escaping America; it's the industries of the future. These are the

Manufacturing Jobs in the United States

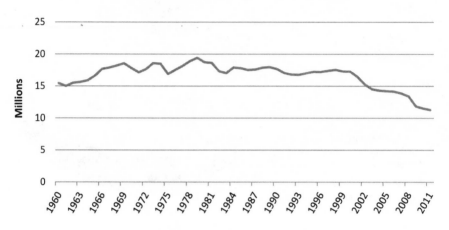

Source: Bureau of Labor Statistics 2010

industries that are essential to make up our economy in the years to come. New innovations and growing modern industries such as solar panels and semiconductors (both of which were originally developed by Americans) *are now being sold back to the U.S. by other countries.* As recently as 1998 the U.S. was the world leader in solar panel production. In 2011 it sits fifth and falls behind each year, possibly falling even farther at the time of this printing.[14] As such manufacturing moves abroad, innovation leaves with it, weakening our national strength, security, and prosperity. If these industries continue to disappear from under us, all we will be left with are much lower-paying service jobs. Are we, as a nation, going to be comfortable with a much lower standard of living?

The only portion of the American population that benefits from the outsourcing of our high-technology goods is a mere handful of corporate owners, frequently foreign, whose profit margins are sky-rocketing thanks to the dip in production costs to record lows as they continue to charge us nearly the same prices. So what is the real impact? The real impact is that if no one has a decent job in America, there will be also no one to buy their goods. A similar short-sighted "maximum profits right now" approach, with no outlook past a few years into the future, is what caused the devastating banking and stock market crisis of 2008. A similar fate looms over us now.

Recently some economic commentators have imagined a post-industrial America where manufacturing would be outsourced to foreign countries and those jobs would be replaced by service industry jobs on the domestic front. (A good example was shown in a prominent article in *The Economist* with the subtitle "Factory jobs are becoming scarce—it's nothing to worry about."15) In such a world, conveniently enough, the disappearance of all industries in the United States would be no problem at all—it would somehow be good for us!

Unfortunately, there are many problems with this projection. First of all, it makes our country highly dependent on imports. Secondly, as studies and real world experience show, where manufacturing goes, innovation follows. This is perhaps most vividly demonstrated by the explosion in the number of American companies and other major companies moving their research and development facilities to places where their manufacturing operations have already relocated.

But there has been another eye-opener: Many lower-paying service sector jobs—where the employee does not have to be present in a face-to-face situation—are equally vulnerable to being sent overseas and are rapidly being outsourced at growing rates. (Witness the constant flow from the market of software professionals, call center employees, and financial advisers whose jobs are now being done in India for a fraction of the cost.)16

While both lower- and higher-paying service jobs such as a company's financial consultants, call center personnel, legal services, and computer programmers and technical support for software are increasingly outsourced, workers in Asia and elsewhere are rejoicing in new jobs and financial freedom as American workers delve deeper into unemployment.

Manufacturing jobs create more jobs supporting the industrial sector while the service sector has much less of a "carry" effect on the rest of the economy. Even though service jobs can be outsourced, they cannot be exported easily. In other words, a person working a service job in our country is not something that can be traded, meaning our trade will become more and more imbalanced in such an economy. Eventually this would contribute to a situation taking us further into debt as we have fewer funds to actually pay for the increasing flow of imports without the profits from manufactured goods we export in return.

Our thirst for cheaper and cheaper products that is served so well by big-box retailers like Wal-Mart and Target is also responsible. For

Two Scenarios of Store Profit Margin

U.S.- Made Good   Cheap Import

instance, Ohio Art Company, which had been manufacturing the iconic Etch-A-Sketch for over four decades in Ohio, eventually had to move production to China to keep the price of their product under $10[17] and therefore appealing to consumers. Moving manufacturing offshore cuts costs tremendously (the CEO of Ohio Art Company mentioned soaring health-care costs as a major reason for their departure) and also lowers the retail price, making a healthy profit for both producer and retailer. But the workers who used to make a good salary in the Ohio factory may now find themselves stocking shelves at Wal-Mart.[18]

We as consumers are responsible for this effect. The allure of cheap goods on offer at big-box stores and elsewhere has been too strong to resist, leading us as consumers to unknowingly undermine our own job prospects and the U.S. economy. Wal-Mart and others were not intentionally setting out to destroy the American economy—they have been responding to consumer demand. This gives us the idea of the effect of the consumer power we have, but it is working in the wrong direction because of a lack of consumers' awareness of the consequences of our actions.

In 2005 an article in *The Economist* stated: "For the first time since the Industrial Revolution, fewer than 10 percent of American workers are now employed in manufacturing."[19] Since 1965, when manufacturing made up the largest portion of the economy, its share has been tumbling to the point where it barely makes up 10% of our economy today. Other countries have also shown declines in manufacturing employment, due to changes brought by mechanization, increased productivity, and lately sending some of their labor offshore, but none to the degree the United States has shown.

U.S. Manufacturing Jobs as Percentage of Total U.S. Jobs

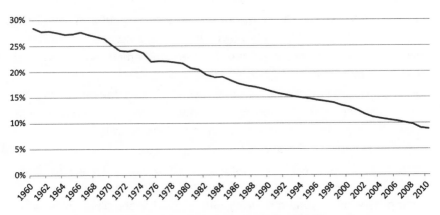

Source: Bureau of Labor Statistics 2010

We have seen our manufacturing base contract at a far faster pace than other countries. Manufacturing share of GDP in the United States has fallen by more than 50% since 1980. In contrast, Germany (22%), Japan (18%), and France (15%) have also seen drops in manufacturing share, but far smaller ones.[20] This is partially due to wise government interference and investment into local companies and innovation, but also *because of their consumer action.* Traditionally, their ordinary consumers have overwhelmingly preferred to purchase higher-quality products made in their own region rather than cheaper products from Asia or elsewhere that they regard as lower in quality. They look at total cost of ownership, not just price at purchase. We stand to learn a lot from this.

Simply put, we have become world-class consumers rather than world-leading manufacturers.

Moving Production Offshore Stifles Future Job Creation and Innovation

In his perspective-shifting book, *Free Trade Doesn't Work: What Should Replace It and Why,* economist Ian Fletcher details a good example of the kind of mistakes that have been made in the manufacturing field in America that led to our current precarious position. He tells the story of Ampex, a small company in Northern California that invented the video cassette recorder, or VCR, in 1970. Then instead of moving it to mass production, they licensed the VCR technology to the Japanese. By doing this, the company managed to collect some millions of dollars in royalties and employed a few hundred people. Fletcher says, "Its licensee companies, however, collected *tens of billions* of dollars in sales and employed *hundreds of thousands* of people." And not only that, but by gathering the know-how and experience in manufacturing this technology, the Japanese also had the inside track on the technological innovations in the field that were to follow and reaped the benefits of future iterations as well.[21]

Richard Elkus, a California based entrepreneur and inventor, also laments the loss of VCR manufacturing and its repercussions for America.[22] The Ampex case was not an isolated incident, but was a part of a larger picture of the United States losing its hold on the electronics industry. The problem wasn't just that Americans lost out on the massive potential profits from VCR production. As a result of the VCR being practically handed to the Japanese, Americans also lost the ability to participate in the design and manufacture of video-recording equipment and essentially all the resulting technologies that came from the proliferation of home video technology. Eventually, the United States basically surrendered the entire consumer electronics industry to Asia. That means millions of jobs and billions of dollars in revenue for both private companies and the government never materialized here in our country. The results are still being felt, for instance, in our now being behind in crucial future innovations such as lithium-ion batteries, first used in cellular phones and now being produced for the rapidly expanding electric car market.

Similar situations have been repeated recently when LCD screen production for televisions moved entirely out of the United States. When new innovations call for touch-screen technology, an obviously massive demand in today's world, manufacturers of those products must go overseas to find companies to make their screens for them since that type of production of innovation simply no longer exists in the United States.

Another more recent example of our loss of competitiveness came with the invention of one of the most successful products of the new century—the Amazon Kindle®. Economist Clyde Prestowitz details Amazon's struggle to keep the product "American" in his brilliant book *The Betrayal of American Prosperity*. What made the Kindle's manufacture possible was a new kind of electronic ink, invented and produced by E Ink Corporation, a company based in Massachusetts. However, although this key part of the product is made here, the Kindle itself cannot be made here because—and this is astounding—most of the components necessary for its manufacture simply *cannot be made in the USA*. Virtually all the other key components of the Kindle are only made in Taiwan, South Korea, China, and Japan.[23]

Each Kindle is estimated to have $185 of value added during manufacturing. But because many of these key components, such as semiconductor chips and batteries, are no longer made in America, it means that only about $40.00 to $50.00 of that value is added in the United States. Prestowitz quotes some analysts who suggest that this number may soon decline to zero, as some believe E Ink may soon move its production and R&D to Asia as well, and not because of cheaper labor but because of other benefits of moving their production there. Friendlier government policies encourage innovation more than the American business environment does by offering more attractive tax policies, fewer environmental and other regulations, direct and indirect subsidies for exports, and government investment into new businesses.

Alarming signs of America's inability to compete in the most crucial industries of tomorrow are everywhere. While the printed circuit board industry was experiencing rapid global growth in the twelve years since the year 2000, it actually shrank in America. Amazingly, that industry shrank in the U.S. from an $11 billion industry to just $4 billion.[24] Our capacity for high-tech innovation is being undermined by the production of such crucial components such as circuit boards leaving the country, taking away potential for future innovation as well as jobs today.

Prestowitz, like Richard Elkus and many others closely involved in American manufacturing, goes on to present the sobering thought that the next E Ink, the next Kindle, the next great innovation, is unlikely to be developed in America because we simply will not have the supporting components or the innovation skills required to create industry-leading products. The battery technology that powers the Kindle and other devices similar to it once was made in America, but left for Asia along with the VCR and nearly all other consumer electronics in the 60s and 70s.

Carnegie Mellon University engineering professor Erica Fuchs examined the effects of outsourcing manufacturing abroad in a recent set of studies. She found that as companies in the optoelectronics field sent their production offshore to Asia, they initially were able to make their products very cheaply and with greater efficiency than they had in America. However, when the companies started to improve their designs and put out newer models of their products, they usually lost a great deal of time when production was offshore. Communication across geographical and linguistic boundaries became harder and slowed things down. Moving only a company's manufacturing offshore markedly impeded the company's ability to stay ahead of the competition in design and production of their new technologies.[25] Eventually the engineers, research and development, and innovators had to move offshore as well to be closer to the manufacturing functions.

Professor Fuchs' studies show the reason why so many manufacturing companies that begin by merely moving their production offshore eventually also transplant their design, engineering, and R&D functions closer to the actual manufacturing facility as well. When this happens, it is the foreign country they have relocated to, not the country of the company's birth, that ends up benefiting. It is that country's young engineers, manufacturers, and designers who learn the newest technological innovations and keys to success, not ours. Eventually, we will be pushed out of the loop altogether.

Harvard Business School studies have shown the same effect. If you move manufacturing facilities overseas, eventually the ability to innovate will be lost as well.[26] The loss of factory jobs may not seem like it will hurt American competitiveness when seen as isolated incidents, but in the long run it has hurt the country enormously.

As companies have been moving their R&D abroad to be closer to their actual manufacturing facilities, incredible statistics have illuminated our need for action. In October 2009 *Business Week* reported that U.S. employment of scientists and engineers had fallen by 6.3 percent, compared to a 4.1 percent decline in overall employment.[27]

In August 2011, NPR's program *All Things Considered* reported that for the first time America, forever recognized as the country leading in innovation, had been surpassed in the number of new patents filed by China. In a *Bloomberg Businessweek* article earlier in the year, famed British inventor James Dyson warned of just that happening and the urgent need for the United States and United Kingdom alike to invest in new innovation. "New ideas are essential because 21st century trade will not be defined by who makes what, but who makes things better," Dyson wrote.[28] For America to retain its status as a leading nation and economic superpower, it is therefore crucial that it retains its edge in innovation and engineering.

The Importance of Balanced Trade

There are two everyday choices we can immediately apply that will boost our economy. One is buying products from countries with which we have an even trade balance, which means an equal amount of exports is going to these countries as is being imported from them. The U.S. has an even trade balance with many countries—the United Kingdom, Australia, and Spain, to name a few.[29] Trade benefits both countries because nations on both sides of trade are supporting their export base with money coming in, and are also gaining access to products they do not have the capacities to produce themselves. As American consumers, buying products from these countries is a healthy exchange.

The other effective action consumers can take is to support manufacturers that specifically benefit their local economy. Let's take a look at how people in other countries make purchases.

According to the French magazine *L'Automobile,* the top 10 best-selling cars in France in 2010 were:

Renault Kangoo	Peugeot Partner
Renault Clio	Peugeot 207
Citroen Berlingo	Reanult Trafic
Fiat Ducato	Renault Megane
Renault Master	Citroen C3

The first thing that becomes obvious is that *nine* of the ten best-selling cars in France are French cars made by French manufacturers. Intriguingly, right next to this ranking in the magazine was a comprehensive list of review ratings given to all the cars sold in France that year. The top ten contained *none* of these cars and, in fact, many of them were in the bottom 20% (and this list had over 80 cars on it!).

What does this tell us? The French buy French cars, even though they know they aren't the best ones on the market. They knowingly purchase cars that may not be as "good" as imports, even from neighboring Germany, because there is some intrinsic value in buying a domestically produced automobile. After all, perhaps there really aren't such huge differences among cars. They most likely will all get you there. These kinds of purchasing patterns will also get their economy there and keep a job there to drive to.

The importance of a strong manufacturing base, as I emphasized before, is that one manufacturing job creates four or five other jobs in the economy, compared to service sector jobs, which only go on to create 1 to 1.5 other jobs. Jeffrey Immelt, the CEO of General Electric, has suggested that manufacturing should make up at least 20% of the workforce.[30] It bears emphasizing: that number in the United States is now down to just 9%.[31] Because of the other jobs supported by manufacturing jobs, the loss of manufacturing base has tremendous effects on local economies.

Buying from countries which expand our trade deficit means we are essentially consuming goods we cannot afford—that is to say, we are taking on debt and selling our assets in order to afford those imports. This isn't just a theoretical point. Assuming the United States has some 230 million adults, as it did in 2010,[32] each person's share of the annual trade deficit adds up to about $2700. That's a lot of money for the average household to shift in its spending. But it is doable in a few years, as more and better products become available with the new shift in demand. Even a very small shift would cause huge ripples in the job market since manufacturers would receive more orders, their suppliers would need to increase hiring as well, and new jobs in retail, transportation, and other service industries would follow. The tiniest shift in consumer spending has enormous consequences because we really are the engine driving our economy.

Some commentators from various free-trade espousing think tanks have continued to suggest that trade deficits don't really matter, even as our economy has visibly suffered as they have grown to record heights. It's absurd. To explain just how wrong this view is, Ian Fletcher demonstrates the problem with trade deficits quite plainly and elegantly. When nations engage in trade they have to give something up to get something else. This is obviously an accepted fact. We cannot expect to get something for free.

So when we buy foreign goods, Fletcher suggests, there are three things we can give in return: goods that we make now, goods made previously, or goods we will make in the future. Essentially, things we make today are goods we are producing and then selling to foreign countries. Previously made things include things such as properties, where no one is being employed in the United States to make them today; we are merely selling off our property to foreign owners. Buying on credit happens when we import goods from abroad in exchange for things we haven't yet made. We promise to give our trade partner something in return later. Essentially, we are racking up debt in that case. But eventually, we all have to pay our credit card bills, even those with the very best credit ratings.[33]

The problems are incurred, clearly, in the latter two options. When we buy imports, and in return sell things we ourselves make for export, this is normal balanced trade activity where each party gets what they require in the trade. When we don't cover the value of what we are buying with what we are selling, we fall into debt and cover the difference with the goods made previously and goods we will make in the future. We sell off existing assets, and take on debt. In Fletcher's words, this is bad simply because *we own less and owe more.*

As legendary investor Warren Buffett put it: "Our country has been behaving like an extraordinarily rich family that possesses an immense farm. In order to consume 4% more than we produce—that's the trade deficit—we have, day by day, been both selling pieces of the farm and increasing the mortgage on what we still own."[34] Buffett also estimated in 2003 that about 5% of our national wealth had already been transferred abroad, a very significant amount, which has surely grown even greater over the years.

Trade deficits are a tremendous problem. We have already reached our federal debt ceiling. We are borrowing a third of our yearly federal budget, an absurd figure plunging us constantly further into debt.[35] Action is needed now, and the more we allow actual asset generating manufacturing operations to leave the country the more staggering our problem will be.

We know that maintaining a manufacturing base with good exporting income is possible in today's world economy. We know that because countries like Germany, Japan, and South Korea are continuing to be strong exporting nations in spite of their higher labor costs, in some cases higher than those in the United States. Many economists, scholars, writers, and politicians have suggested a great many policy changes and trade regulations to turn America's trade deficits around to return the country back to the top of global economy and regain its exporting glory. But as years have gone by the leaders have not taken charge and have not changed direction. Instead they go on creating free-trade agreements around the world that are devastating for our country because they only benefit big businesses that can boost their profit margins by replacing our American workforce.

☆ Chapter 4 ☆

HOW COMPETING COUNTRIES ARE SUCCEEDING

"We cannot survive by cutting each other's hair."[1]
—BERND PFAFFENBACH
State Secretary of Federal Ministry of Economics and Labor, Germany

While many American companies have thrown in the towel on manufacturing domestically, there are other countries where homeland manufacturing thrives, the population is steadily employed, and a sense of consumer patriotism keeps their country's economy healthy. How is it that these economies are doing so much better than ours? Why are their manufacturing sectors so vibrant? How is a country such as Germany, where average worker compensation in the manufacturing sector is $48.00 per hour compared to America's $32.00 per hour,[2] able to compete with the South East Asian manufacturers who pay a fraction of that number? (In China, the average wage in manufacturing is just over $1.00 per hour, while in Mexico, closer to home, that number is $4.00 per hour.)[3] Meanwhile U.S. companies are continually outsourcing jobs, citing high labor costs here as the reason. What are these countries, and specifically their citizens, doing right that we aren't doing?

It is worth looking at some of the industrial policies, intricacies, and general trends in other countries that have managed to keep a strong manufacturing base. Let's examine, for a moment, Germany, Japan, and South Korea in particular. These countries provide examples of model behavior that allowed them to weather any possible economic storm. They point us toward what we can do culturally and in terms of policy if we wish to recreate U.S. jobs and improve our standard of living. What these countries are doing is worth evaluation and, in many cases, adopting into practice. Of course, one could fill an entire book with information about the industrial policies in these countries, and it is not my intention to offer a full-fledged evaluation of their manufacturing sectors. Instead, I am most interested in pointing out that it is possible for an industrialized, high-wage nation to hold on to its manufacturing jobs, and that it is invariably good for the nation, its economy, and its citizens to do just that.

Other examples that I have not elected to cover here include Finland, Sweden, Austria, and Switzerland. These countries vary in their economic structures but many of their policies have similarities to those of Germany, the first of the "model countries" covered here.

Germany: A Case for Aggressive Industrial Production

The strength of the German economy is quite remarkable considering that in spite of the Euro hitting its highest levels in years, Germany is on pace to regain its place as the world's second biggest exporter of goods in 2011.[4] (Since a strong currency should theoretically reduce exports as it makes them more expensive, this success is partially explained by the fact that many of Germany's top trade partners are also in the Eurozone.) This is something truly impressive for a country of 80 million (compared to the 300 million in the U.S.), which was left in ruins and split into two vastly unequal halves just sixty-five years ago. Adding to their impressive current form, in March of 2011 Germany set a new national record for the value of its monthly exports.[5]

At the same time, Germany's unemployment fell under 3 million for the first time in over nineteen years.[6] It is now at its lowest level since the German re-unification two decades ago. This job growth is largely fueled by German manufacturing, helped by their export-leader status and the domestic product preferences of the German people.

The leadership in Germany is clear about its direction and creates policies accordingly. Germany's stated goal of being an aggressive industrial producer and exporter of goods is not just a lofty dream; it is followed by rigorous action on behalf of its politicians, business owners, and citizens to produce domestically and purchase domestic products. The adherence to this attitude has helped the Germans dig themselves quickly out of the recent recession, one in which the United States still appears to be toiling. Germans plan for the long run and what is best in the long-term, not just what will create the highest short-term profits.

Consumer preference for domestic products is part of the way of life in Germany. German car manufacturers completely dominate the German market. They target their own market specifically, tailoring reliable, high-performance cars for the German highways and autobahns. Consumers have grown to trust them, and imported cars from abroad are shunned in favor of domestic vehicles. Indeed, the Volkswagen comfortably beats their own cheaper Czech-made subsidiary Skoda in the German market even though both cars are often perceived to be nearly identical and are essentially made with the same parts. Regardless, Germans are happy to pay the premium for the fully German product, knowing the quality will be top-notch. Premium brand Volkswagen held a 21% market share in 2010 compared to Skoda's 4.5%.[7]

To further highlight domestic manufacturers' dominance, in 2010 the top *twenty-two* best selling cars in Germany were German-made and only three foreign-makes reached the top thirty. The biggest market share in Germany for a foreign car manufacturer is Ford Europe's 6.8% share—and even Ford makes many of its cars in Germany.[8] (In contrast, six of the top ten cars sold in the U.S. last year were Japanese.[9])

This can be seen in many other industries as well, where German companies hold a sizable share of their home country's market—whether in home electronics, power tools, or dishwashers. The people of Germany simply and clearly seem to prefer domestic products on many fronts. For instance, Bosch power tools holds 37% of the German market share and Bosch & Siemens was the market leader in dishwasher sales with a 49% share.[10] The key part of these statistics is that the leaders aren't just German companies on paper—they actually manufacture many of their products in Germany today. When it comes to consumer appliances, German consumers placed a lot of focus on the quality, longevity, performance, and technological features of the appliances they purchased. In particular, the "Made in Germany" logo was mentioned as a specifically encouraging selling point in a 2009 report on the German appliance sector. This included German companies as well as foreign-owned companies who made their appliances in Germany. On a recent trip to Germany I was impressed to see that the cookware and utensils in the kitchen of the apartment I was staying in, from an electric kettle to the can opener, proudly proclaimed they were "Made in Germany." In contrast, the last American factory making silverware shuttered its doors in 2010.[11]

When domestic consumption is high for locally made products, even an export-led economy can survive a bad recession when revenue from exports inevitably goes down.

As has happened in the United States, some manufacturing has been outsourced, but many of Germany's bigger companies still do much of their manufacturing domestically. Manufacturers work together with their employees and the state to ensure that they keep Germans employed. Big government contracts tend to be awarded to German companies that use domestic labor. Giant companies like BMW, Siemens, and Daimler have signed agreements not to reduce their domestic workforce and even to maintain them above a certain level. All of this adds up to a thriving economy.[12]

An interesting example of different consumer behavior in Germany compared to the United States is the failure of the Wal-Mart chain in its attempts to expand to the German market, the third largest consumer market in the world behind the U.S. and Japan. In attempting to expand its retail empire to Germany, the company lost billions of dollars and finally gave up on the market, having perhaps misjudged the German consumers it was trying to sell to. In 2006 the company pulled out of Germany entirely. A study conducted at the University of Bremen on the reasons of Wal-Mart's failure in Germany found that even Wal-Mart's own employees in Germany thought their products were not high quality.[13] Unlike in the U.S., the company could not even provide lower prices than some of their local competitors that German consumers were used to. Refusal of the local customers to purchase Wal-Mart's imported goods was another display of Germany's domestic-oriented culture.[14] While local competitors do offer cheap, low-quality imports much like Wal-Mart does, the populace of Germany is also more willing to pay a premium for locally produced quality appliances and other goods with their savings.[15]

The example of Germany illustrates why manufacturing is vital. In Germany today about 40% of all services are provided for the industrial sector. Let me state that again: forty percent of all services in the country are for manufacturers.[16] The manufacturing sector serves both as the foundation of the economy and what drives it forward. Manufacturing still makes up well over 20% of the German economy compared to 11% in the U.S.

Germany also puts the focus on exports, whereas the U.S. gives emphasis to what we can bring in cheaply. The share of the country's industrial production meant for export has grown from 28 percent to 42 percent in just twelve years.[17] Germany has pushed its products into China and the emerging Asian market, when in our country the traffic in trade flows only one way. Germany's trade surplus adds up to a whopping 7% of their GDP (America's trade *deficit* makes up to 4% of *our* GDP).[18]

Additionally, Germany has kept abreast in new markets such as solar panel and wind turbine manufacturing and is commendable in its ability to foresee developments and stay ahead of the curve. When mechanization took over the jobs manual laborers held before, the Germans started making those very machines that would do human work for them. Someone has to make the robots that make mechanization possible and the Germans began (and continue) to do just that.

Many German companies also conquered niche markets that they can uniquely serve. These companies do not remain complacent about their strong places in the marketplace, but instead continue to develop their products. For instance, Gutehoffnungshütte Radsatz, a company in western Germany, specializes in the development and production of wheels and axles for rail vehicles. They keep "reinventing the wheel," so to speak, to develop better and better versions of their field of expertise. Some of their wheels contain as many as 400 parts, mostly designed and made in Germany, making their end products as complicated as the company name seems to foreign eyes.[19]

Germans have remained competitive with China by targeting the Chinese themselves as customers. German companies, even fairly small ones, have grown into market leaders in products the Chinese want, from drilling equipment to optical mirrors. They are thriving on the back of China's economic success by selling to them and becoming partners instead of employing the more confrontational approach America has preferred (such as demanding that China stop manipulating its currency). The result? Germany's annual exports alone match in value the entire gross national product of India.

Germany has in fact embraced China as a partner, and a rich one at that. China has real willingness to spend money to become a market leader in a number of fields and German companies have gone into business with them with mutual benefits. For instance, in 2010 the *China Daily* newspaper reported that China and Germany had signed deals worth billions of dollars. These included an agreement between Shanghai Electric Group of China and Siemens of Germany to a $3.5 billion project for research and development of steam and gas turbine engines, the signing of a deal worth nearly $1 billion between Ford Motor China and Daimler-Benz to jointly develop trucks in China, and an agreement in place between the two countries of $160 million for green technology development. These kinds of deals seem to be publicized nearly every month.[20]

Rich incentives are provided to companies to keep their facilities in Germany even as labor costs in the nation are as much as a quarter higher than they are in the United States. The German government has specifically and especially supported smaller- and mid-sized companies, which they call *Mittelstand* ("middle size") companies. These companies, characterized by employing less than 500 people, collectively make up 70% of the German manufacturing workforce.[21] The government has established special provisions for *Mittelstand* companies to be able to remain competitive and continue to provide a strong base for the German middle class.

Mittelstand companies include such examples as Windmoeller & Hoelscher, a German company that controls 90% of the world's heavy-duty paper bag production, and Herbert Kannegiesser, the world's foremost hotel-laundry equipment producer. The examples go on and on. These mid-level companies that employ a sizeable share of the German workforce are provided enough capital by the German government and banks to continue to invest in their research and development programs in order to keep the companies on the cutting edge of their respective fields. They see the importance of a happy, productive staff working for the good of the company. Outsourcing the production of their products would cut off the designers from the manufacturers, making oversight of their products more and more difficult. Since middle class engineers and entrepreneurs start many of these companies, few of them want to move all of their operations (and themselves) to Southeast Asia or elsewhere and have plenty of incentive to remain competitive and productive. I can wholly relate to this desire to keep their companies near their homes. It is impossible to imagine a future where *all* manufacturing would move offshore.

Another key policy: Germany does not use the credit system to subsidize short-term consumption as the U.S. does. For example, Germany has remarkably few credit cards per person. This tends to direct lendable money into investment, not consumption. This also tends to favor balanced trade because investment strengthens industrial competitiveness, while consuming more than one produces necessarily means sourcing from abroad (as there's nowhere else to *get* goods if you didn't produce them yourself).[22]

Not only that, but two-thirds of the *Mittelstand* companies borrow their capital from local savings banks—which are legally not allowed to operate outside of their regions. That is to say, these banks only participate in the real, local economies in which they exist. This protects them from the volatile worldwide markets, and they cannot be distracted from their actual business by the temptations of global market fluctuations and investment games.

The success of their economy is a combination of export-led policies, government support for manufacturing and investment, and their citizens preferring to purchase German goods. Instead of spending all of their money and thoughtlessly running charges on their credit cards, Germans prefer to save their earnings. This means they buy fewer of the cheaper, poor quality imported goods and more of the high-quality, higher-premium German, European, and American-made products. And their exporting prowess is equally helpful in keeping their manufacturing base healthy. While Germans are wary of super-cheap imported things, products made near home are often made for specific conditions and consumers instinctively trust these types of products more.

Germany sees the value in manufacturing. This is reflected in reality, in how big a share manufacturing still plays in its economy in spite of paying high manufacturing wages. This shows in its investment in education, and not just higher education. In Germany, professional education from an early age is highly valued, where new trade laborers are trained alongside high school graduates, and where polytechnics and universities of technology are respected and seen as of great importance alongside their universities.

As a manufacturer, I have often found it highly challenging to merely fill positions on the factory floor. There are simply no trained, qualified mold-makers and processing technicians available for our job openings.

Kids in our country are discouraged from having skilled manufacturing careers. They are pushed to college, pursuing liberal art degrees that offer them fewer job opportunities upon exiting. They may then become disenfranchised and labeled as failures or dropouts, and they are bounced around our nation unsure of what to do. In Germany there is not such a strong division of "higher and lower class" professions. Manufacturers need welders and machinists, mechanics and mold-makers, and they are trained (at no or very little cost to the students, I might add) for the needs of their employers.

Japan: Innovation First

Japan became industrialized with extreme rapidity. It used smart state-level planning and the nationalist sentiment of its citizens to become an economic powerhouse with the ability to catch-up to the traditional Western powers, eventually surpassing such traditional leaders as the United Kingdom.

Japan may not be in the most sustainable financial shape at the present since they are lodged even further in debt than the United States. But there are still plenty of worthwhile lessons to learn from the Japanese, given their remarkable economic development, especially during the second half of the 20th century. (It should be noted that most of the Japanese government's debt is to its own citizens who have purchased government bonds, while the U.S. debt is owed to foreign countries. This makes Japan's a slightly "better type of debt.")[23]

Not only did Japan rapidly climb from a relatively "poor" country to a top-tier high-wage, high-earning nation, it is also the second largest holder of U.S. treasury bills.[24] In other words, Japan owns a lot of our country. Until just recently, when China took the lead, Japan was the number one creditor of U.S. debt. As of April 2010 Japan held close to $800 billion of U.S. treasury securities, just behind China, and with about twice as many securities dollars as the number three holder, the United Kingdom.

Ironically, one of the things that was instrumental in enabling Japan to catch up to us in industrial development, trade, and economic power was, in fact, the aid of the United States. After World War II, with Japan in a state of some disrepair and its economy deeply troubled, the U.S. invested heavily in the fledgling country. Our investment along with thrifty and well-focused industrial policies helped lift Japan towards the upper echelon of industrial powers by the end of the century.

In a study published by the U.S. Department of Commerce, titled "Japan's Manufacturing Competitiveness Strategy: Challenges for Japan, Opportunities for the United States (2009)," six key items are detailed which briefly summarize Japan's plan of remaining competitive today and into the next 20 years:[25]

a. using global environmental issues as an engine for economic growth and international contributions

b. doubling investments for education

c. reforming universities

d. increasing investments in science and technology

e. reviewing regulations and social systems with the aim of promoting innovation

f. establishing mechanisms within the government to drive Japan as an innovation-oriented nation

Not only are these goals aimed at growing and supporting manufacturing, they are measurable, clear objectives already illustrated by the makeup of Japan's workforce and business structure.

What Japan is trying to accomplish is clear. Innovation is a word that appears consistently in its plan. Science and technology, i.e., engineering, features prominently. This is essentially a manufacturing strategy aimed at keeping universities and their students linked with the country's future innovation and engineering success. Their goals in their plan to maintain a competitive advantage make it clear that Japan's science and technology plan and its manufacturing strategy are inextricably linked. Innovation without manufacturing is a near impossibility—or, at least, absence of manufacturing from a physical location reduces the speed and effectiveness with which innovation can be expected from that location. If Japan, or the United States, for that matter, wants to continue to have innovation present in their country, manufacturing needs to be retained for that to be possible.

Today, average wages in Japan are as high (or higher) as they are in the United States[26] and manufacturing remains of the utmost importance, as many of the electronics and equipment in our homes demonstrate.

Japan, like all other high-wage countries, has not been immune from outsourcing to lower-wage nations. They have also moved, like all other industrialized nations, to fewer safeguards and protectionist measures in their foreign trade in recent years; although to say Japan now practices "free trade" in the American sense is far from the truth. And it would not be particularly wise of them to do that and to discard all of the lessons and reasons they got to where they now are in the first place—as America seems to have done in the last half century.

In fact, in the 1980s when the United States was actively sending its trade convoys around the world preaching their free trade and free markets ethos to try to get the Japanese and others to open their borders like we were opening ours, the Japanese government instead issued directives to their business leaders specifically instructing them to buy Japanese. Incentives for exports and better rates were provided to their key producers along with tax incentives if they used Japanese materials and suppliers.[27] Essentially what they were doing was trying to create conditions to prevent foreign importing companies from getting into the Japanese market, which would have undermined their own industrial base. If only American leaders had their vision.

It's also not solely the Japanese government that has supported its manufacturing sector. The Japanese people have played a critical part in this as well. Japanese consumers have been shown in various studies to be highly nationalistic in their purchasing preferences, much like their South Korean counterparts. One study presented ordinary Japanese consumers with two products, one was an import and the other was a Japanese equivalent product. The subjects always chose the Japanese product, *even when they knew it was inferior in quality* to the foreign made equivalent.[28] In other words, Japanese consumers prefer domestic products even when they have access to higher quality imports. In contrast, the same study reports that consumers in the United States prefer the domestic product *only* when it is demonstrably superior to competition.

Japanese consumers put much more emphasis on country of origin than American consumers do—perhaps because more things are still made in Japan so they actually have the choice! The top five items for which Japanese consumers especially consider "Made in Japan" to be of special importance are home appliances, food products, cars, medical care items, and personal computers. Among the reasons for selecting

Japanese over imported products in these categories (and others) were durability, familiarity, safety, efficiency, service and maintenance, and ease of use. In the consumers' eyes, these are thought to be superior if the product is of domestic origin.29

An example of how the Japanese can reject cheap imports and foreign goods flooding their market is the difficulty experienced by Wal-Mart during its expansion to that country.30 Much like what happened in Germany, Japanese consumers were not interested in the cheap, low-quality articles from Mexico and China sold in Wal-Mart stores. In other words, with the company's foray into Japan they have struggled to succeed, and Wal-Mart posted massive losses for its first seven years.31 One of the reasons for this is that the Japanese place a high premium on quality, and since they earn fairly high wages they do not have a problem with paying more for better-quality products. Wal-Mart, however, has been determined to keep going in Japan, after pulling out of South Korea as well as Germany.32

This is not to pick on Wal-Mart. Clearly it is one of the world's most successful companies, a company that has created its success with hard work and identifying what consumers want: everyday products at slashed prices. But the backlash against Wal-Mart overseas perhaps signals these two countries' shared values. These are values Americans used to possess, too, and could again learn from. Our simple, everyday actions are very powerful and conceding any more control of our country to massive multinational corporations and foreign governments that care little about those of us who are "average people" is a great mistake. It barely needs to be said: this should not happen.

It's not just the Japanese people who prefer their own products.33 (An interesting fact is that some researchers have found that Japanese people do not *solely* put a preference on domestic products.) What Japan has been unusually successful with is creating a nearly worldwide image of Japanese manufacturing excellence. Top Japanese brands and even their products with no name recognition are some of the best-valued products in the world because consumers in countries across the globe believe that Japanese-made products are of high quality and consider them extremely desirable. In developing countries like Thailand or Malaysia as well as the Netherlands and the United States, Japan, as a country of origin for products, ranks highly in people's minds.34 This is quite a goal to reach since in the 1960s Japan was still considered a nation that made cheap toys and other "imported junk"—not too far from the reputation China currently has. Now China is aggressively growing and taking similar steps to those of Japan fifty years ago.

Massive electronics companies like Mitsubishi, Toshiba, Panasonic, Sony, and many others have been at the core of Japan's rise to the top of the economic sphere. Semiconductors, an essential part of any electronics manufacturing, are a key component to manufacturing in Japan, making supply chains for electronic manufacturers more manageable. Japan has worked hard at this, much as China has done recently. Their major manufacturers have suppliers readily available at close distances and they can easily communicate to their suppliers as well as their assemblers, making the manufacturing process more streamlined and easier to manage.

This tells us that Japan, like Germany, has built a successful industrial economy based largely on exports and domestic consumption. The Japanese have managed to create a highly successful web of exports and trade around the world, including the most important markets today: China, the EU, and ours. The U.S. carries a nearly $100 billion trade deficit with Japan.[35] Brand knowledge is extensive and Sony and Mitsubishi have a strong market prescience in Europe as well as in America, Asia, and South America. Japanese tech producers do have many of their products assembled in China since labor there is much cheaper, but they source a bigger portion of their components and parts from within Japan. Indeed, the "American" Apple iPod has more Japanese than American parts in it.[36]

Any developed nation has its share of income inequality and, with that, a poorer class of people as well, but this is less pronounced in Japan where CEO pay, for instance, can be as low as 5% of that of the comparable American level.[37] In contrast to their American counterparts, Japanese directors of companies do not take out exorbitant stock options or tremendous compensation packages. Furthermore, Japanese CEOs are expected to actually run a successful company while our executives reward themselves handsomely regardless of how the company actually performs. From the top down, Japan is committed to strengthening innovation in order to boost their manufacturing economy. They know that the health of their economy relies on it.

South Korea: Long Term,
Sustainable Manufacturing Growth

If we are trying to rebuild the American economy, a country like South Korea is of great interest to us. It is a nation that built an impressive manufacturing base from the ground up in a relatively short period of time. As recently as 1961, South Korea's average yearly income was only $82.00 per person. To put that into perspective, the average South Korean in that year earned less than *half* of what the average citizen of Ghana did ($179.00).[38] This could be attributed, in part, to the incredibly destructive Korean War that split the country into North and South Korea. Half of Korea's manufacturing base was destroyed during the war, along with 75% of its railways.[39] But a long local history that kept much of the population spread out in agricultural and fishing communities, combined with destructive Japanese colonial rule, had also kept the Korean citizens poor.[40]

All of this makes South Korea's recent rise into the top tier of global economies even more remarkable. Today, South Korea is the world's seventh largest exporter[41] —and it accomplished that with very few natural resources of its own. In just five decades the country's average wages have risen steadily and per capita GDP has risen from $700.00 in 1965 to $19,000.00 in 2008.[42] Today, manufacturing makes up 25% of South Korea's labor force, with services making up 68% and agriculture just 7%.[43] This kind of explosive growth has a number of factors behind it, and chief among them is a national strategic investment into manufacturing and a population willing to buy into domestically produced goods. Exports increased in value from $40 million in 1963 to $96 *billion* in 1994.[44]

A national concerted effort started by top figures in government was formed in the 1960s and 70s to specifically create manufacturing facilities geared toward export of labor-intensive goods. The South Korean economic development was a long-range project that no one in the country expected to work instantly. They knew it was a long-term mission. During that time the South Korean government also set up a number of R&D centers to develop their industrial base.[45]

The South Korean government supported and protected certain industries in manufacturing with a view towards catching up to the leaders in various fields in the rest of the world. These industries included shipbuilding and automobiles, and later on high-tech electronics, which was something the rest of the world viewed incredulously at first, but which turned out to be a huge success story for the country. Exports make up nearly 50% of the GDP in South Korea.[46] This compares to 11% in the United States,[47] making the country both highly successful in its attempts to climb into the top class of export-oriented service and manufacturing powers in the world and highly dependent on continued demand for its export products. This is why South Korea is not complacent. Their leaders know not to just rest on their laurels, but to continue to push into new fields and industries of the future where they work to remain as the world's top producers of things like renewable energy equipment, electric cars, and semiconductors.

South Korea now produces 17% of the world's semiconductors, a major industry that many expect to grow even bigger in the future.[48] A new semiconductor wafer-fabrication plant costs upwards of $8 billion to build and creates thousands of direct and indirect jobs. These jobs are not just temporary jobs, since for a company to make such a massive investment it can be expected to remain in that location well into the future. South Korea has built an impressive presence in the field, has enviable expertise, and is the third largest semiconductor producer in the world today, having only begun its foray into the field in the 1970s.[49]

In the 1970s and 80s, the country also became a major force in shipbuilding by making oil tankers and oil-drilling platforms.[50] As of 2008 Korea held 50.8% of the global shipbuilding market including ownership of Europe's largest shipbuilder, STX Europe.[51]

South Korea is now the world's fifth largest automobile producer.[52] Much of the demand originates from within the country, giving it a solid base to produce its cars. Ninety-nine percent of the cars driven in South Korea are South Korean-made. With a population of less than fifty million, South Korean manufacturers still produce nearly a million vehicles every year—a testament to their exporting power. With such a loyal populace ready to purchase the domestic vehicles, coupled with government limitation on imported vehicles, the South Korean carmakers had a solid platform on which to build their exporting operation as well. In 2010 South Korea exported $53 billion worth of vehicles, their second most significant export behind electrical equipment.

The country was able to avoid the global financial crisis of 2008, one of the only developed countries not to be severely affected by it, thanks to stimulus measures and *strong domestic consumption of products* that compensated for the drop in exports. In the short term, South Korea's nationalist consumer tendencies (electing to buy domestic whenever they could to support their own nation's economy) made up for a potentially calamitous drop in exports.[53] In contrast, in times of economic difficulty, Americans are often urged to go shopping and to consume more, but since most of the products they end up buying are imports, the money just flows out of the country and this creates extremely little long-term stimulus for the economy. No manufacturing jobs are created when this occurs, and these jobs are what really form the backbone of an economy as they create other jobs to support them. In South Korea, however, the opposite is true because domestic products are favored to imports at all times and the country, in effect, supports itself even when other countries hit rough patches when they can't buy as many imports.

The story of South Korea's rise seems to be a collection of unlikely events. Samsung, South Korea's largest exporter and a massive global corporation today, started out in 1938 exporting fish, fruit, and vegetables before branching out to refining sugar and producing products in the textile industry. In the 1970s it moved into the semiconductor business in a move that was widely ridiculed and invited shrugs of shoulders around the world. For over a decade the company subsidized its fledgling electronics division with the profits from its textile and sugar operations. Eventually it became a giant in its field, surpassing many of the companies, political leaders, and, one might even say, entire countries that initially passed them off as silly. Samsung's success story is similar to that of Finnish communications giant Nokia, which lost money on its electronics division for its first *seventeen* years before taking over the cell phone markets around the globe. Nokia, like Samsung, was at the time mostly making money in logging and the manufacturing of rubber boots.[54]

This type of long term commitment to manufacturing is illustrated by many South Korean companies. Hyundai began in the automobile industry in 1967; it took seven years to produce its first model of car. Amassing the know-how, technology, and skill required to be a major market player takes time, and the Koreans understood this.[55]

South Korea also made major changes to its education system, first by working tirelessly to improve the levels of literacy that were extremely low in the country in the 1960s, and then in the mid-70s by opening up the South Korea Institute of Advanced Science, a graduate school of engineering and applied science. It also established new schools in mechanical, civil, and electrical engineering at existing universities, as well as numerous other new science programs in order to nurture a new generation of highly educated engineers and scientists ready to take South Korea to the top of the high-tech development wave.

Cambridge University Economist Ha-Joon Chang, a native of South Korea, writes vividly about his experiences growing up in the 1960s during the emerging of a new South Korea in his wonderful book *Bad Samaritans*.[56] He talks about the unique perspective gained from living in a country that in only a few decades progressed from a developing nation that was on an economic level with many African nations to a bona fide industrial giant with living standards largely comparable to that of the Western world. How this was accomplished is a story that in many ways mirrors the success of Samsung.

Chang remembers his school years as a teenager when he and the other kids were instructed to turn in any of their friends who they knew were smoking foreign cigarettes. The country was making a conscious effort to sponsor its own manufacturing by frowning upon the consumption of foreign goods. Living at a time when foreign-made cigarettes were taboo evokes for Chang strong memories of his excitement when discovering some American or French cigarettes at a friend's house. This kind of strongly-imbued consumer nationalism is one crucial practice in South Korea's industrial rise.[57]

Various writers and anthropologists who have studied South Korea, including Dr. Laura C. Nelson of Stanford, point out the South Koreans' strong sense of national identity was and is a propeller out of poverty and into prosperity. They have an exceptional pride in their country that means they want to be successful in their endeavors and want to be viewed as successful from the outside as well.

Dr. Nelson traveled to South Korea to study consumer nationalism in that country specifically. She quickly got an interesting insight of what "country of origin" means to South Koreans when she decided to purchase a clipboard for conducting her interviews. She spent some time picking the perfect one, of a nice color, not too expensive, and firm enough for her purposes and that seemed durable as well. She mentions that many South Koreans admired her clipboard as she talked to them—and every single one of them asked whether it was made in Japan or in South Korea.[58]

The average South Korean is unusually interested in where things are made and whether they are domestic products. In this case, she thought they were also probably curious because they perceived it to be a high quality product and were hoping it was domestically made and not an import from their neighboring competitor, Japan. Indeed, the first person who noted the clipboard was a government employee, who upon learning it was from Japan, mentioned that the board was "very nice" but that she would never buy it since there must certainly be one much like it that was made in South Korea.

It wasn't just her clipboard that got people's attention. Almost every item Dr. Nelson had on her solicited the same question from the locals: "Where is it made?"

Asking that question in each of our homes elicits a familiar response. Go ahead; check the tags on things in your kitchen, your living room, your bathroom, and your garage. Where are your possessions made? If your house is like mine, or the average American's, not a lot of it is made here. If you have been wondering why our country's economic and social progress appears to have stalled for 90% of us, there's your answer.

Chapter 5

THE LABEL GAME

"Figures don't lie, but liars figure."
—MARK TWAIN

Most of us are not entirely sure where any of the objects of our everyday life are manufactured. For example, let's say you wanted to know where the shirt you are wearing was made. There might be a tag on it indicating "Made in India." However, if your shirt has buttons, they may have been made in China. The thread holding the seams could have come from Egypt and the tags and cloth from Vietnam. The tag that indicates "Made in India" is only part of the story. All things considered, the shirt you are wearing probably has four countries of origin. In fact, though the shirt may have been assembled in India, perhaps not one single component of it came from India except for a small portion of labor. When it comes to the information we are provided about a product's country of origin, we are grossly, some might even say dangerously, misled.

Egypt   China

Vietnam

MADE IN INDIA

You may not have even been able to locate a tag on your clothing that indicates its country of origin. Often companies will go to great lengths to make that information as inaccessible as possible. At this point, you ask yourself, "Why is this such a big deal? Why would companies want to keep us in the dark? And, why should we care about where things come from?"

Most companies aim to maximize profit. Some do this honorably by creating a quality good or service in an ethical way, while still being savvy enough to manage the bottom line. However, a lot of businesses tend to take another route: outsourcing to the cheapest source possible, making products which have only the appearance of quality at the time of sale. In many cases they outsource their entire manufacturing operation. They attempt to maximize their profit margins by shipping off their labor to countries with low labor costs that may also have lax human rights, few labor laws, and poor environmental standards. This act of outsourcing has not only inflicted on consumers an abundance of poor quality products. It has put Americans out of work, the very same Americans manufacturers then rely on to purchase their products. This has dramatically increased their short-term profitability, but, as you've seen, has wreaked deep and lasting damage on our economy. The only way to incite a change strong enough to turn our struggling economy around is a consumer movement. We must pay attention to what we purchase if change is to happen.

You might be thinking: "Yes! I am on board. I want to be more aware. Sign me up! How do I do it?" This is where a critical problem must be exposed: you cannot currently adopt this approach because the current information we are provided on a product's country of origin is either misleading, incomplete, inaccessible, or all of these.

Current regulations require companies putting out products to list only the country where the "last major transformation" of the product took place.[1] Essentially this means goods that are manufactured, assembled, designed, and packaged in several different countries, or that have multiple components from suppliers in different countries (like the example of the shirt earlier in this chapter) are wholly misrepresented as to their country of origin. Take your cell phone, a product that most of us rely on every day. Your cellular phone might have been designed in the United States, have components made in South Korea, Japan, and Taiwan, and then have been assembled in China. The final product will simply say

"Made in China," leaving out information that may have discouraged or, alternatively, encouraged you to purchase the product.2 (Don't bother looking for that "Made in USA" cell phone, though—there aren't any!)

Many American consumers are naturally drawn to products that can be identified as "Made in the USA." After all, it is in a citizen's best interest to support local economies—they provide jobs and, in turn, income that re-circulates and bolsters the local economy. Companies that qualify for the "Made in the USA" logo typically display it prominently for these very reasons. Also, products made in the United States have a reputation for quality because of strict manufacturing standards. The Federal Trade Commission (FTC) oversees use of the "Made in USA" label, but it does not have an active enforcement unit that regulates or calls companies out on false use. The FTC relies on consumer alertness to identify products that falsely claim to be made in the United States. How much time do you have to devote to the task of discovering whether the "Made in the USA" label on the product you just bought is misleading? And, where would you begin in order to get to the bottom of the mystery?

FTC regulations state that in order to qualify for the "Made in the USA" label, a product has to be "substantially all" made in the USA. This is defined by its regulations to mean the following:

- "The product was last substantially transformed in the United States and U.S. manufacturing costs are at least 75% of total manufacturing costs; OR
- The product was last substantially transformed in the United States and all significant parts or components of the product were last substantially transformed in the United States."3

Needless to say, this last definition is more than a little vague and leaves it somewhat open for corporations to interpret in a way that best suits their marketing objectives. Most companies with any sort of marketing savvy realize the lure of branding a product as "American." And they have complete freedom to capitalize on the name "America" or any word or image associated with the country (think American flag) in order to better sell their products, regardless of whether any part of the product was actually manufactured or assembled in America.

Look at the board game Scrabble. Packages of the famous game have a "Made in USA" label on them. But what does that mean? A CBS News article figured out that its racks, tiles, and letter bags are all made in China.[4] This led CBS to conclude that only the board itself and the packaging were American-made. Still, under the current federal regulations, this is a "Made in USA" product.

According to the FTC, "A brand name alone, even one including the word 'America' or a city or state, does not constitute a made-in-America claim."[5] This fact creates a wide open space for companies to mislead the consumer in multiple ways without us even batting an eyelash. Take the popular "American Girl" dolls found in many a young lady's bedroom in this country. These pricey dolls, despite their name, are produced in China.[6] At the grocery store a package of mushrooms proudly proclaiming "America's Favorite Mushrooms by Pennsylvania Dutch" oddly enough comes from the same country as the dolls.[7] On a recent trip to Costco, I purchased a pair of socks with the brand name Sheffield Socks. Sheffield is a famous town in England. Aware of the historical quality of English textile, I chose that particular brand. At home, looking closer at the packaging, the truth was revealed: "Made in China."

The company Pennsylvania House Furniture cuts down trees in Pennsylvania, ships them to China to be fashioned into beds, chairs, and so forth, and has the finished product shipped back to the United States for sale.[8] Their website makes no mention of this process or anything related to the manufacturing of the furniture, but it does include a lyrical section on their history, making specific note of using American cherry trees of the highest quality. Not surprisingly, none of the products showcased on their website shows country of origin information.[9]

Countless companies intentionally mislead the public with confusing brand names that suggest the product comes from one place when it is actually built in another. Why wouldn't they? There are no rules against doing this and if it helps sell their product, why not take advantage of it? I recently visited a home improvement store and picked up a shovel that announced "Still Made in America" in prominent text written on its packaging. But as my wife with her younger eyes discovered when we got to the check-out, tiny text hidden in the back of the product revealed it actually came from China! I, like so many of us on many of our purchases today, felt cheated. How can this be legal? The prominent, accessible text turns out to be simply the trademark for the brand, and not a country of origin claim made according to the regulations of the FTC.

Rob Weylan, manager of a store called "Made in America" in Elma, N.Y. that proudly stocks only 100% American-made products, also expressed frustration at the looseness of FTC's rules in an NPR interview from 2011. He spends hours investigating products his store carries to make sure that they really are 100% American-made, a time commitment that is unfortunately necessary because of the looseness and loopholes contained in FTC's "Made in USA" labeling rules. As a patriotic store owner of integrity, he wants to make sure that his store, named "Made in America," actually and truly only carries products made in America.[10] Right now, labels don't tell the whole story. He, like you and I, would have to go to all his suppliers individually to establish where all the components come from.

Examples of misleading country of origin information can be found in abundance in stores across our country. Luxury brands like Prada, Armani or Burberry have recently been moving more of their production to Asia.[11] An American Public Media article from 2009 points out that these brands still highlight their glamorous European heritage in their advertising, even as more of their products are manufactured with cheap labor in Asian countries. The article stated that Giorgio Bonacarso, a chemical supplier for the shoe industry, claimed that 9 out of 10 top European brands at that time quietly made their shoes in China.[12] Producers in some cases make most of the product in China and then ship it to Italy to be finalized—in which case it will have a "Made in Italy" tag on it. These products typically retail for ten times more than the cost to produce them.[13] The customers who trust in the value of a big luxury brand are buying goods that may be partially or completely made in Asia, believing the brand is still all-European made. Some Italian luxury brands, desperate for that legitimizing "Made in Italy" tag, have even had their products made in Italy by illegal Chinese laborers.[14]

Companies not only have the freedom to be misleading. They can also offer terribly confusing and vague information to the consumer. Actual labels such as "Assembled in the United States from domestic and foreign components" tell us some labor has been done in the U.S., but gives us no information on *where* those components come from and what percentage of work is actually done here.

Some companies have come up with creative ways to mislead consumers. Sara Bongiorni, author of *A Year Without "Made in China": One Family's True Life Adventure in the Global Economy*, gives a humorous account of a family's attempts to avoid purchasing and using Chinese-made products for a year. On one of their shopping trips she encounters sunglasses that announce they were made in "Panoceanic China" and "Transoceanic China."[15] This is evidently to mislead the consumer into thinking the glasses aren't "Made in China," but perhaps in other countries. For the record, these "countries of origin" mentioned on the labels do not exist on maps.

While consumers face a lot of misinformation about a product's countries of origin, sometimes information is simply not available in any form. This is the case with catalog and online shopping. Consumers who shop by catalog, mail order, or on the Internet often cannot peruse a product's package. They buy at their own risk. Furthermore, companies are not required to put one iota of information on a product's country of origin on the display page. There is simply no way of knowing where anything you buy in a catalog or online comes from until it arrives at your doorstep, and even then you will be partially (if not totally) in the dark. Forrester research suggests that web sales in the U.S. will reach about 11% of all retail sales by 2015, with that number growing to 15% if you exclude groceries.[16] Essentially, millions of dollars will be spent shopping online, where consumers are not required to have any access to information regarding country of origin.

The world's largest online retailer, Amazon.com, has no country of origin information on the products it sells. Amazon.com does list the exact dimensions of a book, the name of the publisher, the language it's in, its weight, number of pages, and all kinds of additional information related to the book. Details, some might even say minutia, are included, but nothing is included to indicate where the book was actually printed. Amazon.com sells a huge number of other types of products, from wiper blades to sewing machines, and again gives tremendously detailed information on the size, weight, and contents of these products, but in almost all cases the country of origin information is omitted.

What benefit do these companies stand to gain by keeping us in the dark? What are they afraid we might find out? And would it affect their bottom line? Nike, facing growing public scrutiny over the working conditions of its employees in third-world countries,[17] was one of the first major companies to release complete listings of its factories on its websites.[18] Levi Strauss soon published a similar list on its website of its factory locations. Or, to be more accurate, it published a list of its subcontractors' factory locations, since Levi Strauss doesn't actually make anything itself! It has subcontracted all of its production to other companies that are in about fifty other countries.[19] Levi Strauss released this information to be more transparent about its manufacturing process, mainly in order to ease the concerns of those customers worried about the conditions in which the company's products are made. And it worked. Listing the locations of those factories where the production is subcontracted is a good step towards openness. But consumers only have access to this information if they seek it. In other words, it is not easily accessible when you need it: at the point of sale.

Patagonia, an apparel retailer marketing itself as an ethical, environmentally aware company, has gone even further than such companies as Nike and Levi Strauss and releases the exact steps many of its products take during production. From the gathering of source materials, to the sewing, and to warehousing, a potential customer can see exactly where its garments come from. If a consumer were to have concerns about workers in China having been exploited in the making of his or her product of interest, he or she can choose another product. Patagonia stands out as an exception in a sea of missing information and misinformation. But its action reveals how valuable country (or countries) of origin can be to a consumer trying to make sound decisions.

The examples of Nike, Levi Strauss, and Patagonia lead us to a question: why haven't other companies published this information? Perhaps because, as a representative from the Investor Responsibility Resource Center says, there simply "isn't enough public pressure" on companies to have formal company codes relating to labor issues.[20] This obviously extends to country of origin and the true origins of their products as well. The aim of all of these companies is to convince consumers to purchase their products. If consumers demanded (and, in turn, considered) more information on country of origin as a prerequisite for purchasing a product, a lot of companies might have to make real changes in the way they currently do business. A consumer movement to persuade Congress to pass new laws about product labeling information can affect change and stimulate companies to produce this information.

The demands of consumers are taken seriously by manufacturers. For instance, the athletic shoe manufacturer New Balance now provides a comprehensive listing on their website detailing exactly which of its shoes are made in the United States, which ones are assembled or only partially made in the U.S., and which ones are entirely imported.[21] This kind of transparency ensures that the consumers will not be confused or come out feeling cheated when making their purchases and enables us to make educated choices. New Balance should be commended, not just for still making shoes in the United States, but also for the way in which it communicates this to its customers today.

Chapter 6

INFORMATION YOU NEED WHEN YOU NEED IT

"Information is the currency of democracy."
—THOMAS JEFFERSON

The very essence of our government is predicated on transparency. Information regarding the allegiances of our politicians and the bills and propositions that could alter our lives is vital for a true democracy. The privilege to vote would be a moot point if we didn't have access to pertinent data to help shape our decisions.

Voting is the ability to take an active role in the decision making that affects us individually and our communities. It is useful to imagine the other areas of our lives, outside of the scope of politics, where we "cast a vote" in favor or in opposition of an issue. For instance, riding a bicycle to work instead of driving a car is a vote in favor of preserving clean air and protecting natural resources. Instead of just saying a cleaner environment would be nice, by changing a habit you actually contribute to the shift, making your decision that much more powerful. In this sense, every purchase that you make is a vote—a decision that should reflect your personal values and your hopes for your community. Buying a product without knowing information about it would be like making a trip to the polls without having researched for what or for whom you will vote. The problem is that as consumers we have significantly less relevant information easily available to us than when we vote for our leaders. And, as we've explored, much of this information is vague or, in worst cases, false.

We are undermining our own safety nets, including our national security. Our military and government agencies have recently publicly decried the difficulty of acquiring components and equipment that are made in the United States. It probably requires no explanation why it would be harmful for our national security if our military contractors and government planners would need to import the parts necessary to build essential military equipment. With the chance of a conflict, we simply cannot depend on getting these parts from overseas.

How Labels Help

Historically, adding forms of labeling on product packaging have addressed a myriad of issues that occur when consumers lack necessary information. Labels are used to convey nutritional information, health and safety standards, use of fair labor practices, and many other types of data or certifications that the average shopper will find useful, even necessary. Most products display some country of origin information, but I have shown how the current model is misleading and detrimental. The entire point of including the label on a product's package or tag is to place information in the hands of consumers when they need it—right at the point of purchase, where most people will examine it. Few people do extensive research on each item they intend to purchase before going shopping. Detailed, less confusing, and unambiguous country of origin labeling is an essential step towards consumers making educated decisions that will help our economy as a whole, as well as each of us individually.

Country of origin information already exists when it comes to grocery purchases. Many consumers are especially interested where our food comes from because it directly affects our health and our pocketbook on a day-to-day basis. With recent health scares from tainted foods imported from foreign countries, namely China, pressure grew to enact binding legislation to definitively state where our food comes from. In 2002 a bill was introduced in the U.S. Congress designed to include country of origin information on certain common food products such as beef, fish, produce, and nuts.[1] Tireless lobbying pressure from the food industry parties kept the bill from being implemented until 2008. During this time, polling consistently showed widespread consumer support for the bill. International polling firm Zogby, for instance, found in 2007 that 88% of consumers surveyed wanted all retail foods labeled with country of origin information. Not only that, the same polling firm also reported that 95%

of those asked felt they had the right to know the country of origin of the foods they purchased.[2]

This seems reasonable as today *nearly two-thirds of the fruits and vegetables consumed in the United States come from overseas.*[3] Just as impressive, more than three-quarters of the seafood we consume also comes from foreign countries.[4] This piece of information is included in a *USA Today* article from June 2011, which discusses the Food and Drug Administration's intention to team up with foreign regulators to make sure the food coming to our shores is safe. These plans are not solid, however, and collaboration between the FDA and twenty foreign government agency equivalents certainly requires money as well as probably years of negotiation. The FDA's own budget has been slashed due to the poor shape of our economy. Since we now have country of origin information on our foods, we should use it wisely. The FDA can only inspect about 2% of the food imports coming into the United States since its resources are overwhelmed by the rising mass of imports.[5] We can see directly where our money is going only when we purchase American goods, especially when purchasing meat, dairy, or fresh produce. Supporting your local farmers and retailers who sell these goods is supporting your own community.

Food labels have had a twofold effect: consumers feel safer knowing where the food they eat comes from and also make choices that help their local economies by redirecting money to nearby producers when in the past many of these funds have gone overseas. In recent years, a movement to support buying local foods has gathered much momentum as more and more people have (a) come to believe that food from local sources is more trustworthy, (b) hoped to support local farms and producers, and (c) recognized the potentially devastating environmental effects of importing food from afar where production is less regulated than in America. Today we can make choices at the supermarkets to support local farmers by buying American-grown produce instead of imported goods. Without labeling these choices are impossible to make without going straight to the source (for instance, farms) to purchase our food. If food has country of origin labeling, why can't all other consumer goods?

Consumers today are more scrupulous when it comes to their everyday purchases. People want to know if the food they are buying contains unhealthy ingredients that may trigger an allergic reaction. This information has not always been available, but it is crucially helpful to those trying to make conscious decisions regarding their diet and those carefully avoiding ingredients they know will cause health problems or allergic reactions.

In 1990 it was decided that consumers had a right to know nutritional information for the packaged food they purchased so they could make informed dietary decisions. (See figure below for an example.) Food products in grocery stores now contain detailed labels listing all ingredients, the nutritional information about the food, and the possible presence of eight of the most common allergens in the products (including milk, eggs, and nuts). These labels did not appear out of the food producers' friendly desire to provide as much information as possible to consumers.[6] They were born out of the Food and Drug Administration's decision to require labeling information in an effort to curb the obesity epidemic in America and to give information about other diet-related health problems that had escalated at alarming rates.

Nutrition Facts
Serving Size 1 cup (85g)   (3 oz.)
Servings per container 2.5

Amount per serving	
Calories 60 Calories from Fat 0	

	% Daily Value
Total Fat 0g	0%
Saturated Fat 0g	0%
Cholesterol 0mg	0%
Sodium 55mg	2%
Total Carbohydrate 10g	3%
Dietary Fiber 3g	12%
Sugars 5g	
Protein 1g	

Vitamin A 300% - Vitamin C 5% - Calcium 3% - Iron 0%

* Percent Daily Values are based on a 2,000 calorie diet. Your daily values may be higher or lower depending on your calorie needs.

	Calories	2,000	2,500
Total Fat	Less than	65g	80g
Sat. Fat	Less than	20g	25g
Cholesterol	Less than	300mg	300mg
Sodium	Less than	2,400mg	2,400mg
Total Carbohydrate	Less than	300mg	375mg
Dietary Fiber	Less than	25mg	30mg

Calories per gram Fat 9 - Carbohydrate 4 - Protein 4

The provision requiring the packaging to announce the presence of any of the eight most common food allergens was added in 2004.[7] The Nutrition Information and Labeling Act law is subject to strict regulation by the FDA and all food packaging must contain all this information in a way that can be easily interpreted by consumers. We are accustomed to seeing this information in a form that is largely consistent throughout all food packaging. Nearly everyone can agree that this information is highly useful for all of us. And if you don't think so, it is easy enough to ignore.

Just as consumers have a right to know the properties of the food they purchase, we should also have clear, consistent information that would help us make informed decisions with respect to country of origin. We can check and compare a food product's nutritional data before we buy it, and we should have the same access to country of origin information at the point of purchase. And not only should you see the last place where the product was manufactured. You should be able to discern what portion of its components came from other places. Consumers deserve and need a total picture if they are to exercise their purchasing power in an influential way.

Companies use tricks to make you think their products are American when they aren't by using brand names or logos to mislead you. All of this implies that these companies themselves already know that country of origin is important to the consumer. They know consumers value certain things in products, so they exploit those values in their marketing.

Let's say you are interested in a fine pair of Italian shoes. As we mentioned in the previous chapter, some manufacturers of luxury goods in Europe and elsewhere are making their products "on the cheap" in other countries and claiming they are made in Italy, thus justifying the ever-increasing prices of these products. So you may be disappointed to learn when you order shoes from a company located in Italy, with an Italian designer and an Italian brand name, that the shoes are actually manufactured in China. Chinese-made shoes usually have less of a prestige factor than expensive Italian shoes. But the manufacturers make more money by claiming they are "authentic Italian shoes," creating a connection to a century's long art of cobbling in Italy. I know people who are in the shoe manufacturing business. They claim that the Italian-made shoes actually are better made and will last longer than Chinese ones. So the "brand name" companies who have moved away have a double win: they make more money on the shoes and get to replace them more often.

Country of origin matters because manufacturing matters. The stability of our economy relies on it. When we buy imported products, we support industry somewhere else. This may be good or bad, depending on circumstances. It is certainly good in that when we buy products from other countries, we create trade with them. There may be something we make that they will be interested in. Of course, for trade to be balanced, we need to be making something good that they aren't. However, our trade *isn't* balanced. Disproportionate amounts of imports are flooding our country and are destabilizing our economy, and the structural base of our economy: the industrial sector. This is particularly true of our trade relationship with China.

I have been to China numerous times and have seen the situation first-hand. The people have different preferences, and cultural differences often mean the things that are successful here may not be equally popular in China. There is also a sense of national pride that means they prefer to purchase locally made products rather than imports. There are exceptions, as the popularity of Apple's iPods and iPhones in China has demonstrated. But other companies that have completely cornered our market, such as

Google, are fairly marginalized in China where local competitors lead the way.[8] Of course, in addition to the cultural barrier, there is a language barrier—things built for consumption by English-speaking people may work differently from what the Chinese are used to with their very different language. Whatever the reason is, they are not buying many American goods.

One of the few areas where the issue of country of origin has been directly addressed is the automobile industry. The American Automobile Labeling Act (AALA) was enacted in 1992 to give potential purchasers of automobiles in the United States additional information to help us make educated choices in buying cars. Consumers now have access to information regarding where a car and its components are from. The legislation requires all cars to have labels displaying the percentage of American/Canadian parts content, the country of its assembly, as well as the country of origin of the engine and transmission, two key components of any automobile (see figure below). This label is not a complete listing of country of origin of all car components. All cars contain many more parts than listed in these labels. But, each label is a good primer for buyers to see where their cars come from. Any car with less than 70% American/Canadian content is classified as an "import." On the other hand, any car over 70% American/Canadian content is "domestic."[9]

Motor vehicles have had country of origin labeling for nearly twenty years now. While the effort to do this is going in the right direction, many

---

PARTS CONTENT INFORMATION

FOR VEHICLES IN THIS CARLINE:

U.S./CANADIAN PARTS CONTENT   50%

MAJOR SOURCES OF FOREIGN PARTS CONTENT:

JAPAN   20%

FOR THIS VEHICLE:

FINAL ASSEMBLY POINT: XXXXXX, OHIO, USA

COUNTRY OF ORIGIN:

ENGINE PARTS: U.S.

TRANSMISSION PARTS: JAPAN

NOTE: PARTS CONTENT DOES NOT INCLUDE FINAL ASSEMBLY, DISTRIBUTION, OR OTHER NON-PARTS COSTS.

people don't even know the label is there, so it hasn't been as helpful as hoped. But if they knew to look for it, they would find interesting things.[10]

Countries of origin labels often reveal unexpected information. There are people who want to support the American economy by purchasing domestic products but have suspicions about the quality of American cars. In examining a country of origin label, it might be revealed, for instance, that the Japanese company Toyota makes a number of their models in the United States. The Toyota Sienna is assembled in the U.S. and 83% of its parts are of American or Canadian origin.[11] Toyota has numerous factories in the United States that manufacture its cars for the American market,[12] as do German manufacturers for the production of the BMW[13] and Mercedes Benz.[14] It is not ideal for the American economy for people to purchase products manufactured by foreign companies on U.S. soil, but it is much better than buying outright imports. People in our country *are* getting paid to make these cars, and these foreign companies are creating jobs and wealth in the United States—something to take into account when making purchases, but only possible to know if country of origin information is available.

It is not the case that products need be 100% American to benefit America. Every percent you can increase in U.S. content adds up, even if it is only a minority of the total. If 10% of a product's components come from the United States, this helps a number of suppliers making those components and it means there is 10% less labor and value that would be outsourced. Of course, as it stands, there is no way for us to know if any product is "10% Made in USA." Labeling laws do not require or even allow for such specifications. Including the percentage of content in country of origin requirements would enable this type of specific, valuable information. This often benefits manufacturers as well as consumers.

Different types of labels include certifications from expert agencies, such as certifying foods as "organic." Also common are labels identifying products that come from low-wage countries that use fair labor practices, letting consumers know that the people making those products were paid proper wages. Most of us have seen the *fair trade* logo on our shopping trips. Big companies like Starbucks, conscious of public demand and eager to project an image of corporate responsibility and sustainability, have begun using ever greater quantities of fair-trade-certified coffee. The stamp is awarded by a single certifying agent, Fair Trade USA, and it gives consumers a certain confidence that their money is going to the workers responsible for getting the product to them in the first place, instead of to the already overflowing coffers of massive global corporations.

The "Made in USA" label is not so different. We all know the difference in wages in the United States and in Cambodia or Vietnam. Some low-level employees in textile or assembly lines in Asia may be paid as little as 30 cents an hour (often even less in smaller, less prolific factories for companies with less name recognition).[15] These employees may get no benefits and are often asked to work extremely long shifts with very few, if any, days off. When they complain or fall sick under the workload, they may be replaced immediately. In the United States there are laws and protections in place for employees so that they cannot be exploited in such a way. Factories are inspected to make sure no abuses take place. When you buy a product that says "Made in USA," the intention is to inform you that you can be sure that the worker has been fairly compensated and is working in humane conditions. This is another reason we need to make sure that labeling is accurate: products that say they have been made in the United States should actually be made in the United States.

We need to be able to trust that "Made in USA" claims are accurate. For a product to be labeled "Made in the USA" it must meet the Federal Trade Commission's requirement that 75% of value has been added in the United States, or has had its last "major transformation" occur in our country, but the manufacturer may have utilized illegal immigrants to make components that are transformed into the final product. That remaining percentage of certain components could have been be produced by labor outside the country and is "hidden" from the consumer. We know "Made in USA" doesn't necessarily mean "100% Made in USA," but it is impossible to say where parts come from.

Labeling solutions have been developed before to solve problems of misinformation or to weed out deceptive marketing strategies. The labeling solution I am advocating has a similar goal. Information is necessary for democracy to work—Jefferson was well onto this idea during America's inception as a democracy. If we—citizens, consumers, voters—do not have all the information in our hands, we cannot make educated decisions. Getting you the information you need when you need it is what this book is all about. Get ready to meet a new and improved country of origin label that can change the course of our economy.

☆ Chapter 7 ☆

THE TRANSPARENT LABEL

This chapter is the crux of the book: a solution. It presents a method for placing vital, complete information regarding a product's country of origin, including the nationality of the manufacturer and their current trade ratio with the United States, in the hands of the consumer at the time of purchase. It will also cover ways you might use country of origin data to make more informed buying choices. Your dollars not only have the power to purchase. They have the power to incite change on a global level depending on how you spend them.

As we have shown, simply showing the country of origin as the place where the last major transformation of the product occurred is incredibly incomplete and misleading to consumers. When making a purchase we need access to information regarding all countries where components were manufactured and assembled. By having a clearer picture that such a label would provide, we can make better buying decisions—decisions aimed at rebuilding our economy and supporting other countries that practice balanced trade with the United States. A user-friendly, more informative label might look something like this:

COST BY COUNTRY		
ORIGIN	%	TRADE RATIO
USA	37	1
Canada	30	0.90
Taiwan	15	0.73
China	8	0.25
India	8	0.65
Mexico	2	0.71
CO. Registered in Delaware, USA.		

Label 1

Or like this:

COST BY COUNTRY		
ORIGIN	%	TRADE RATIO
China	80	0.25
Vietnam	8	0.25
Japan	4	0.50
Taiwan	3	0.73
Egypt	3	3.05
Thailand	2	0.40
CO. Registered in Delaware, USA.		

Label 2

You'll immediately notice that these labels give a much more complete picture of a product's makeup than an indiscernible, difficult-to-locate sticker or tag that simply reads "Made in Japan." If we are to make informed buying decisions, accuracy is essential.

If you are conscientiously trying to purchase goods in order to support American manufacturing, you will notice that neither of these products is "Made in USA." However, Label 1 tells you that 37% of the product's value came from the United States, whereas Label 2 tells you the product was entirely made abroad. Assuming these are otherwise totally comparable products, buying the first product will be more beneficial for the U.S. economy, considering it was at least partially made here.

Another detail contained in the labels is the location of the manufacturer's headquarters. Both of these theoretical examples are from a company located in Delaware, United States. Therefore, even though the product described in the label in Label 2 is produced overseas, at least it is from a U.S. company. This means the manufacturer pays taxes to the United States, as probably do its managers, marketing staff, designers, and so forth. A hypothetical third product that is made outside the U.S. by a foreign-owned company is another comparison, which would result in even more money flowing abroad.

Just how would this label work to educate the consumer? As you can see, it provides exact percentage of value added to the product by each country of origin. A product that is completely sourced in America and assembled by American workers will have 100% of its value added in the United States, and therefore the label would simply have that one country of origin. If that product—let's say its entire production cost is $100.00—were to have one component ordered from Mexico that cost $2.00, the label would read 98% United States, 2% Mexico. This is a simple calculation of where the money was spent in the making of the product.

As a manufacturer of products for over forty years, I know for a fact that establishing these figures is not difficult. If some company claims this is prohibitive or expensive, it is probably merely trying to cover itself, not wanting to disclose these numbers for fear of public pressure. If, indeed, a company markets itself as patriotic and makes nothing in the U.S., perhaps it should worry. If a company claims not to know exactly where its parts come from, it is either lying or completely incompetent. It writes the checks and pays someone to get its goods made. Its executives know where their money goes.

The third, extremely important detail in this label is something you should be wondering about. It is the item called **trade ratio**. As you can see from the example, the trade ratio next to Mexico says 0.71. This is a simple figure which you get from dividing exports to Mexico with imports from Mexico. A figure below one means America imports more from the country in question than they import from us. Following are charts showing the fifteen nations from which the United States imports the most and the countries' trade ratios with the U.S.

Why is the trade ratio useful? Because balanced trade benefits this country greatly. You can see that the trade ratio we have with the United Kingdom is close to 1.0. This means that money we invest importing goods from that country gets re-invested in the United States in almost equal measure. Therefore, trade with that country is beneficial to both parties. You can feel good about purchasing a U.K.-made import because the money you send over there by buying their product gets reinvested in the United States by the British purchasing in equal measure from American companies. Even replacing a purchase from China at a .25 ratio, with one from South Korea at .79, is a huge improvement. A healthy, balanced trade ratio is one close to 1.0. In part two at the end of the book in our Consumer Travelogue you will find a comprehensive listing of our nation's trade ratio with most of the countries in the world we import from, with notes on specific countries also listed in the travelogue.

Top 15 Countries U.S. Imports from

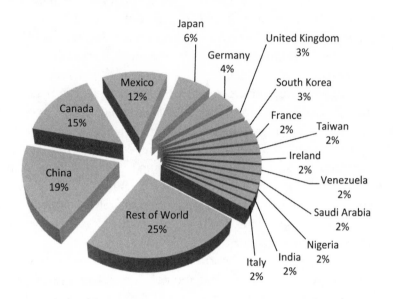

Source: United States Census Bureau's foreign trade statistics 2010

Trade Ratio of Top 15 Countries U.S. Imports from

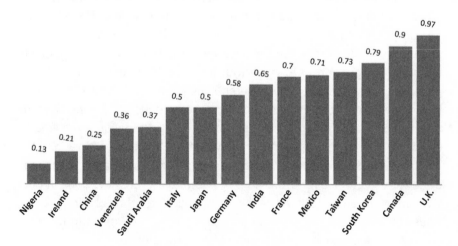

For example, you will see that Nigeria is a country we import a great deal from, but we export nearly nothing to the country. This is mostly because a vast majority of what we import from Nigeria is oil. The money we spend importing oil from Nigeria then stays there—that is to say, Nigerians do not invest that money in buying products from the United States. This is an extreme kind of skewed trade ratio, but it helps you to clearly see just how badly the importing of oil hurts our economy.

Country of Origin as a Useful Indicator

Just as important as accuracy is accessibility. For the label to work it must be consistent, and consumers need not only the ability to review it when they are considering a product in a store, but the ability to review it when making catalog and online purchases. Guidelines indicating what consumer goods must be labeled and how they are to be labeled should be strictly enforced, but should not be overly burdensome to the manufacturer. The ultimate goal is to apply consumer pressure on companies in order for them to see a direct, profitable benefit in relying on American labor and components. Your purchasing decisions are that powerful.

Country of origin information can be utilized in a variety of ways. It presents benefits for the consumer, benefits for manufacturers that strive to make products in this country, and benefits for national economies when they fall into favor with the consumer. The label reveals where the consumer can find quality goods from specific locations or it can be used by the consumer to make choices that support national economies—both in America and other countries that practice balanced trade. It can help consumers steer clear of purchasing from countries with poor humanitarian, political, or environmental records. The label can also give consumers the information needed if they want to purchase products from countries with strong records that need economic support to grow the countries' industries and better provide for their citizens.

The following explores some of the benefits a country of origin label provides for the consumer, manufacturer, and nation, and how you can use the label to exercise your buying power.

Knowing Country of Origin Can Guide You
Toward High Quality Regional Goods

Certain countries and regions are known for exceptional craftsmanship of particular goods or services. Their mastery of production rightfully turns consumers toward their wares. There are several historical examples of this: Swiss watches, Italian shoes, Japanese cameras, French cookware and wine, German automobiles, and English textiles.

If a consumer were devoted to buying, for instance, the best bakeware, French companies would be a consummate starting point. After all, the French are known for their delectable and high-quality baked goods. A recent browsing on the Internet led to a site that marketed itself as a French cookware company. After ordering cast iron cookie sheets (the French are renowned for this product), I received the cookie sheets. A small sticker on the package indicated the famous French cookie sheets were, in fact, "Made in China."

One of the benefits of having a worldwide, regulated "country of origin" labeling system (that is also enforced on Internet purchases) would be the elimination of this type of misrepresentation in marketing. If consumers truly desired French cookware, not "French-style cookware" made somewhere else, they would have easy and clear access to this information. One of the best arguments for the label is marketing integrity. Why should you spend your hard-earned cash on something you have inaccurate information about? And why should you be lied to?

All this is not to say that consumers should give a cold shoulder to emerging industries in countries not previously known for producing a product. Who is to say Indonesia won't sometime in the future actually make superior cookware? The benefit from proper country of origin labeling would give the consumers more information to decide for themselves, perhaps supporting such shifts in consciousness. If the Indonesian cookware is identified clearly as being of Indonesian origin and consumers become more aware of its quality, this could prove a boon to the cookware industry there. More importantly, the labeling would significantly reduce the opportunities that companies now have to purposefully misrepresent the origins of products. It would be practically impossible to try to advertise a product as being from a certain country when it was mostly manufactured elsewhere if the label indicated this right on the product itself.

WHO'S MAKING YOUR ELECTRONICS?

You may have heard of a company called Foxconn in the news over recent years. It got a string of bad publicity in 2010 when a number of the company's employees committed suicide in their industrial complex in China.[1] This company, also known as Hon Hai, has a massive manufacturing presence, mostly in China, but also in other low-cost locations such as Mexico, Brazil, and India.[2]

Foxconn manufactures consumer electronics for companies such as Amazon,[3] Apple, Intel, Nokia, Microsoft, Dell, HP, Sony—essentially all major corporations whose gadgets fill our homes. In fact, Foxconn alone employs more people than the worldwide number of employees of Apple, Dell, Microsoft, HP, Intel, and Sony *combined*.[4] Foxconn is now China's largest private employer with over 1.2 million workers.[5] In all likelihood, if you have an electronic device from one of these companies, it may have been made by workers at Foxconn—and certainly not in America.

Buying on Ideological Principles

In our world, money rules. Decisions are made mainly to maximize profit. Money is power, on scales both large and small. Huge corporations and substantial governments make critical decisions on how large sums are spent. These decisions, in turn, create the climate of our lives. You may wonder if how you spend your money can possibly incite any significant change in the world. Step back for a moment. Every huge corporation caters to the consumer and works to earn your favor—from offering things at lower prices, appealing to you through clever marketing schemes, and branding itself and their products so you will recognize them. If huge corporations believe in the power of the consumer, why don't we, the consumers, see this power?

What I'm describing here is a consumer revolution—a reclaiming of our ability to effect change through our spending habits. This would have consequences felt around the globe. There are many different approaches we might take in how we choose to spend our money. Mindful purchasing can only be made possible if we have the information we need to consider our choices.

Manufacturers will provide the kinds of products that people want to purchase. There has recently been a lot more information available to the average consumer about what types of food are healthy and which ingredients they should avoid to remain healthy and avoid common diseases. Manufacturers and retailers have responded to public demand by creating more and more "healthy" products that do not have certain unhealthy ingredients, for instance, products that proudly proclaim "no artificial sweeteners" on their packaging. The largest retailers and chains like Starbucks also have responded and are even introducing their own lines of "healthy foods." Because of nutritional and ingredient labeling requirements, the companies are forced to a degree of transparency that makes it very difficult to mislead consumers. Claiming a product is a "healthy" and nutritious choice when it may contain high amounts of unhealthy ingredients is difficult, since the manufacturer would essentially be revealing its marketing lies right there on its own packaging labels.

Making informed choices about food only became a reality when nutritional information became accessible to the consumer. We have a lot to learn from this moment in history when the nutritional values were required at the point of purchase. Individuals can use the values to determine a variety of things. If you are concerned about sodium, you can examine a broth's sodium content in relation to recommended daily values. If you are avoiding gluten, the information that you need is in the ingredient list. Just as we all take different approaches to determining what food we will eat based on health concerns and differing values, the same sense of individuality can be employed when purchasing non-food products if you have access to country of origin. Your decisions can be made in favor of supporting a certain country's economy, avoiding purchases from a country with poor records in human and/or environmental rights, or, conversely, rewarding a country with an equal trade balance. Below are some examples of how you can use the information contained on the "country of origin" label to affect certain outcome.

Many people make their purchasing decisions based on personal ideologies and beliefs. Take my daughter Leslie. She is what you might call a soft-hearted environmentalist, even going as far as starting her own small eco business, HankyBook, championing her environmental ideals by making a product she invented to make handkerchiefs more user-friendly. She takes great care when making purchases to be certain the items are produced in ways that are ecologically sustainable and "good for the earth." Many of these decisions are made a great deal easier for her because of labeling on products. If a product says "Made in China," she might consider that the Chinese Environmental Protection Agency only employs about 300 people, versus 17,000 in the US,[6] leading to enormous pollution problems (estimates suggest only 1% of the Chinese city-dwelling population is breathing air that is deemed safe).[7]

She has also been with me to Shenzhen, China and seen the unbelievable air pollution. Also coming to her mind may be the 6,871 miles between her home in Southern California and China, where many of our most common household goods are manufactured. Things made closer to home obviously have lower transportation costs and emissions, something an environmentalist might take to account when shopping. She will also take care to note whether a plant-based product, such as a clothing accessory or a bathroom mat, is from organically grown plants, something ascertained by a certified label. Another point she would look at is whether the products were sourced and manufactured using Fair Trade practices. For many of us, it is important to know that the products we use every day were produced using fair labor, to know that people in distant places weren't being abused and taken advantage of when they made our goods for us, and to know they were paid fair wages for their work. This is something a Fair Trade label assures us. At the present time, a huge variety of products, from coffee to cotton pillows, display the Fair Trade label.

A lot of people harbor positive memories of countries that have made an impression on them personally, such as vacation in Morocco, a study-abroad year in Denmark, a work assignment in the Far East, or a trip to the country of the roots of their family. They are likely to be more aware of the kinds of things that these countries manufacture and seek out products that support their economy, especially when a country they like is a poorer nation and its people could use our dollars. In America there are hundreds of little shops on hip city streets dedicated to selling wares made in African, Asian, or Caribbean countries by creative and productive people in those nations. With a country of origin label, perhaps these people will also be able to support their favorites in ways that would surprise them, for instance by buying goods that contain Moroccan raw materials that they previously thought were entirely Indian-made.

Similarly, consumers with strong views can choose to boycott products from nations they feel need to be sent a message. In the late 1980s and early 1990s a consumer boycott on products imported from South Africa to oppose the apartheid government was able to build a strong groundswell of support. Eventually this consumer movement (along with official and worldwide pressure and strong work within the country of South Africa to change attitudes) led to government action here and an international trade embargo against South Africa, which finally caused the apartheid regime to collapse.[8] This is, of course, an extreme example of how consumer action can lead to positive change. It is also a powerful reminder that what we buy, or don't buy, can cause a shift in a government's policies and laws.

Labeling Benefits to Manufacturers

An interesting perk for reforming labeling would be that it will clarify contents for manufacturers who consider the "Made in USA" label a marketing advantage. If a company has to date had 40% rather than 75% of its product's value added in the United States, it has not been able to make the "Made in USA" claim for its product. This leads to the vague labeling like "Assembled in the U.S. of Foreign Components" that awakens suspicion among consumers. Because any shopper interested in supporting American industry will see a shoe that is 40% made in the U.S. as more desirable than a shoe that is 100% made in China, this would give American manufacturers the opportunity to flaunt their domestic credentials and encourage them to increase domestic content for conscientious shoppers who might be thinking "The more American the better."

One company for which confusing and vague "Made in USA" labeling rules have probably been detrimental is the New Balance shoe company. It maintains five factories in New England as well as one in the United Kingdom for the European market and is very proud of being the only "athletic" shoe manufacturer still making shoes in the U.S.[9] It is also the only major company manufacturing its shoes in the United States [10] and today makes about 25% of its products domestically.[11]

The rules have been forcing this company to use statements like "Assembled in the USA of domestic and imported materials" or "Made in China of domestic and foreign components." This is all unclear to the consumer and gives no perspective on exactly how much of the shoe is coming from each country. These rules do not allow the company to advertise its partially foreign-made shoes as partially American, even though a good portion of the value of the shoe is added in the U.S. In a way, this might be seen as encouraging the company to then make either all or none of their shoes in the U.S.

Being able to mark its shoes as 30% or 40% American would certainly allow New Balance certainly more flexibility than the current legislation that only allows "Made in USA" labels on products containing more than 75% American materials.

Percentage content labeling would clarify these types of situations greatly. New Balance and other companies that partially manufacture products in the USA have argued in the past that the "Made in USA" label provides a competitive advantage without which there is "no incentive to produce in the USA at all."[12] This becomes an issue for the American company that in order to remain competitive or when simply needing certain components unavailable here ends up with portions of its product from other countries, effectively denying its right to the "Made in USA" label. Changing to a label that clearly states exactly how much comes from the U.S. and how much from elsewhere, consumers would be able to tell what was made where. Sixty-five percent American-made is still an attractive proportion for a consumer looking to support American manu-facturing when a competitor product is 100% made overseas.

Chapter 8

MAKING EVERY DOLLAR COUNT

"America will always do the right thing,
but only after exhausting all other options."
—WINSTON CHURCHILL

et me jump ahead several years to the future. Better yet, come with me. Picture this: our foreign trade is balanced. In fact, there is a trade surplus. Unemployment is manageable. Job seekers are finding jobs that suit them and where their skills are valuable and needed. New technologies are being developed all over America, creating new positions for workers who are engaged in appropriate training that addresses the evolving technologies. People are again employed in positions where they are making things for good pay.

Exports are soaring. Citizens in foreign countries are regaining faith in American products. The "Made in USA" label on products instills confidence in the quality, longevity, durability, and honesty of American goods. Greater revenue is enjoyed by new manufacturing companies and jobs are created to support those companies. Smaller- and medium-sized manufacturers that service the small- and medium-sized markets through supply of parts, materials, and expertise are prospering. Service industries are busy serving the well-compensated workers at these high-tech plants. A growing number of accountants, lawyers, salesmen, food professionals, and others find themselves in demand thanks to the growing number of manufacturers employing people at good pay.

If this sounds like a future that is attainable, perhaps that is because it already happened once during our lifetime. This scenario describes the year 1970—the year before we reported our first trade deficit in 1971.[1] Of course, not everything was ideal. We were engaged in another costly war overseas and our citizens were frightened about an external threat creeping into our lives. Sound familiar? Perhaps costly wars and fear of a threatening country are constants in American life. But the rest of it sounds pretty good to me.

A lot of things have changed since then. We live in a different world now. The Soviet Union may have fallen, but China has taken the role of an Eastern challenger for our leadership in the global economy. We still make more things than anyone else, but our share of the pie has become smaller, our lead has been cut, and the profits from our labors are going to the financial operators at the very top at the expense of our middle class. Globalization, outsourcing, off-shore manufacturing, corporate efficiency, financial engineering, the preponderance of multinational corporations in our lives—these are all things that have markedly changed our world in the last forty years. But the basics of prosperity are something we can get back to. We cannot lose sight of what made us successful in the past, and it is not such an enormous challenge to recreate it in the present. The rebuilding starts with *you*.

We, as consumers, can begin the change ourselves. We have long practiced informed elective democracy; now we must add informed economic democracy to our daily routine. We must actively inform ourselves and make purchasing decisions by considering the economic impact of where our money is going. We have long been waiting for someone to do it for us, or more accurately, have been distracted from the problem. Politicians, elected leaders, financial "experts," and economists all suggest solutions that could change the fabric of our economy, but it is really we, the consumers, who are the power that can initiate the change. This power is located in the sum of our buying decisions. Our climb back to the top begins with where you spend your next dollar.

A large portion of the trade deficit is created by consumer spending on imported goods (including indirect purchases such as components and parts of goods ordered by American businesses from abroad). Because not all imported goods are equal, it would be remiss to apply a boycott on purchases of all foreign goods. Sometimes buying an American product is more expensive than buying an import in a meaningful way. That is to say, buying an imported freezer will save you hundreds of dollars, maybe a thousand, because there is only a very small industry left in the United States manufacturing those products, making them too expensive for most people. Buying an American-made cell phone or television is even more challenging, mainly because they do not exist. I am not advocating a wholesale "Buy America" campaign. We do not need to, and should not, shun imports entirely and categorically. But there are huge differences among the imports available. Some have U.S. content; others come from countries with which we have balanced trade. Lastly, you can be mindful by purchasing from a corporation *based* in the United States. At least its income tax will go into the U.S. Treasury.

What I am talking about is shifting a portion of our disposable income from imported goods to American goods. Or, in a more flexible way, to choosing products with the most American content and giving preference to imports from countries with better trade ratios. Because current country of origin information on packaging is so misleading and unspecific, our renewed labeling requirements will greatly help consumers steer the economy in the direction they want it to go. It is like a change in eating habits to improve your health. A splurge now and then can be great, but our everyday purchases need to average a change. This consumer movement will not bind anyone to do anything; it merely gives us all more information to make educated decisions. And, perhaps, this extended transparency will also encourage manufacturers to go to more American or equal trade countries' suppliers when it is possible.

As a manufacturer myself, I am very much aware that in many cases American suppliers are presently prohibitively expensive to the degree that using them will price you out of the consumer goods market. Most Americans won't pay a huge premium for slightly higher quality or domestically produced products. But I can also testify that the majority of warranty repairs for our products come from the minority of parts we have purchased from overseas. These suppliers have regularly substituted cheaper materials than those specified, left off parts, and even used counterfeit parts in assemblies. If consumers would look at the total picture and pay a little more for a longer-lasting product, we as manufacturers could afford to pay a little more for content that helps *our* economy and gives you years of service.

If we only shift a small portion of our income toward American-made goods, we can turn the entire economy around. We would be foolish to look to Wall Street and expect the bankers, investment firms, and speculators to save our economy. That was our mistake in the first place. Their purpose is to make the maximum profit possible. They do not care where they employ people; they merely care that those people create profit as cost-efficiently as possible. We have traded in engineering ingenuity—real manufacturing—for financial engineering. Only we ourselves can guarantee our security, stability, and prosperity.

We can set the year 2030 to be the year to restore America to the financial security it had in the 1950s and 1960s. Of course, that came on the heels of World War II, after which all of our competitors were in shambles. When somewhere in the world is cut, a part of America bleeds. We empathize because the vast majority of us have roots somewhere outside North America. We helped them get back on their feet and had the luxury to have this largesse. Then the United States, with only 5% of the world's population, produced half of all manufactured products. Presently, our 5% of the world's population produces only 20% of the world's goods and we are in financial turmoil. We can no longer afford this level of generosity.

Other countries also had a high demand for our goods. This was because our products outshone all the rest. Why aren't our products the best anymore? Put simply: we no longer make them ourselves. There's no difference between the cheap, anonymous Chinese product and the American brand-name product that is now manufactured in China. All of our concern and focus changed to manufacturing products that were cheap and easily available, with little care for quality and durability. But doing that has undermined our own prosperity. Ironically, as we have gone for cheaper and cheaper things, we have made ourselves less and less able to afford them.

Wages have stagnated for Americans, except for the richest 10%, for the last thirty years. Most of us make less money now than we did in 1980, if we consider that comparing the amount we earn now should be calculated with an adjustment for inflation. Companies are outsourcing their workforces and firing American workers, and at the same time their CEOs rake in record compensation packages. Nowhere is this more obvious than on Wall Street, but the Wall Street disease has infiltrated our traditional manufacturing companies as well. Before the financial crisis in 2008 General Motors was making 80% of its profits through its financial arm.[2] This arm was originally created to offer financing for people buying cars, but as time passed, GM became involved in the same kind of trading, speculation, and other financial engineering as the rest of the Wall Street firms that were so removed from reality. This behavior was the source of the recent meltdown. GM had to be rescued by the government and, even then, instead of using our taxpayers' bailout money to create jobs at home, it outsourced jobs to Mexico.[3] If even state-owned companies don't keep American workers employed, we as citizen-consumers are the only ones who can ensure that there are still jobs here in twenty years.

With more information spreading among our citizens, Americans are seeing the value of investing in American-made products. We have learned from tough times that it is a good idea to save and not buy junk you don't really need. It's better to invest in a high-quality product that will last ten to twenty years rather than in a new, cheap product every two or five years. And it's better to buy locally than give your hard-earned money to a foreign country that will spend it on overtaking us in manufacturing, and on buying bigger and bigger pieces of our country as we sit and watch until there is nothing left that we own.

Our trade deficit is over $600 billion. There are 330 million Americans. That means if each adult American spent about $3,000.00 a year on American goods (or goods imported from equal trade partners) instead of spending it on countries we have highly negative trade balances with, the trade deficit would just . . . disappear.[4] Of course, spending $3,000.00 a year on goods is a big change in many people's buying habits. However, if it were possible for Americans to shift their purchase choices to reach that average $3,000.00 amount for each person, it would create almost 8 million jobs in America. Even if you just began to redirect a fraction of your spending towards domestic goods, together, we would create a lot of jobs.

Imagine what would happen if all these companies suddenly noticed that Americans were beginning to buy more "Made in USA" and less "Made Abroad"? If we each shifted purchasing, let's say, $100.00 per month of things made in a country with a bad trade ratio such as China to American-made, this would make a $200 billion dent in the deficit. That's 2 million more Americans employed in manufacturing. These are jobs created without stimulus money from the federal government. They wouldn't have to be paid for by budget cuts, higher taxes, or increasing the federal deficit. These employed people would be paying taxes, not drawing unemployment checks. America's economy would get healthier.

A huge shift like that would create more demand among American companies for American-made goods. More suppliers would find their parts in demand and need to hire more American workers. Any small movement like that would have tremendous long-range effects. Companies noticing demand for more American goods would deliver just that, and would buy American parts instead of foreign parts to bring manufacturing back to the U.S. Before you know it, the trade deficit would fall and millions more Americans would be employed. We could have all that by each American spending just $100 less per month on imports, and buying American or equal trade partners' goods instead.

Writing this book has made me, as a consumer, look a little harder at labels. And it isn't as difficult as one might imagine. For instance, last weekend my wife and I went shopping for clothes. Because we now look at labels, we changed our decisions from buying the first thing we picked up and liked to one we liked and was also made in the United States. Surprisingly, we found excellent jeans and shirts that were comparably priced with imports and made here. When we can't find American products in stores, we search the Internet. It's kind of fun, like a scavenger hunt.

Consider, for example, what happens if one person decides not to get an imported Nissan, and instead buys an American-made Ford or a Toyota manufactured here. That's a $20,000 purchase and a $16,000 content shift to the United States from just one person. Consider that the replacement parts will probably be from the U.S. as well, further supporting American jobs in the future.

There are already hopeful signs. A *Bloomberg Businessweek* article in May 2011 suggested that many American businesses are beginning to hire more people back in the United States—not to suggest they are rehiring all of their lost jobs, but a fraction of them are coming back right now.[5] Some estimates show that in a few years it may not even make economic sense to manufacture things in Asia since their wages are rising and their currencies are gaining value. The article quotes an assessment from the Boston Consulting Group that wages in China in 2015 will be as much as 69% of those paid to comparable workers in Mississippi.[6] Factor in the costs of transportation, the delays in production caused by geographical distance, and possible patent violations, and it starts to seem like we can successfully compete, particularly with our smaller companies who primarily serve the domestic market.

Of course, if production leaves China, who is to say it will come back to America? Vietnam, Malaysia, or another emerging economy may well continue to make things more cheaply. But there is hope that some of the millions of jobs we have lost in the last decades will be returning. As consumers, we can make that happen.

Indeed, smaller companies that never left the United States are seeing the benefits right now. With our big corporations flooding Chinese factories with orders, these factories are beginning to even turn down business from the U.S., particularly small orders. This is to the benefit of many small American companies who are ready and willing to accept the orders.[7]

Bloomberg Businessweek in March 2011 reported on Boathouse Sports, a Philadelphia-based manufacturer of apparel that was working at full capacity even in the current "everything is made abroad" economy. The article tells the story of a Dartmouth College rugby coach who when facing a quickly-approaching spring season was still without uniforms for his team. So, he found the Philadelphia-based company who could fulfill his order in a fraction of the time Asian companies quoted to him—and for approximately the same price. Small businesses drive our economy, much like consumer spending drives those companies.[8]

Still, more action is needed, and the situation will not easily correct itself. There will always be low-wage countries where their labor is cheaper. And, as Alan Tonelson, a research fellow for the trade group U.S. Business and Industry Council, says in relation to the good news about increases in manufacturing here, "There's a very big deal being made out of a few anecdotal instances. I think it's a lot of wishful thinking going on."[9]

What isn't wishful thinking is confidence in consumer ability to help recover the American economy to its previous strength. Mark Andol, owner of the Made in America store in Elma, N.Y., points out that there are a myriad of things that are still made in America. After all, he's managed to fill his entire store with 100% American products.[10] From jeans to toilet paper to nuts and bolts, these items are available to purchase at fully competitive prices, and they are available not just in this specialty store. We need to support these products and these companies that have made a commitment to America by choosing to buy from them.

Perhaps we need to steer away from not only the manufacturers that sell our job positions overseas for higher profit, but also the retailers that encourage this practice. Wal-Mart is now the world's largest corporation.[11] It holds immense power because so many of us shop there, and have bought into the cheapest goods available, unaware of the consequences. Wal-Mart is the largest toy seller in America.[12] What their customers want to buy is what stores and manufacturers will supply.

The continuing drive in America cheaper products, such as the Ohio Art Company's decision to close its U.S. factory and move production to China, is causing long-range industrial degradation. Had the public's buying habits been to purchase American-made toys for slightly higher prices, the workers making Etch-a-Sketches would be working today.

The fact that Wal-Mart now sells "organic food" at slightly higher prices means that Wal-Mart can be moved to offer goods at slightly higher prices, as long as we know to demand them. We hold the keys to the economy and we, as consumers, create most of the economic movement in this country. Wal-Mart and other retail chains may be powerful, but we made them powerful by shopping there. The reason as much as seventy percent of Wal-Mart's products are from China is that we have wanted to purchase them.[13]

America must once again produce as much as it consumes. We then will have a robust economy with plenty of stable, well-paying jobs. But it will require another American movement to create this. Americans have made the investment to protect the environment, eat healthier food, and travel in safer cars. We now need to invest in our economic future.

We, the American people, with our everyday purchases, can choose to return this country to the prosperity it once had. We have the freedom to choose where we send our money, and where that money goes has tremendous influence in this world.

Let's use that power. We can create a promising tomorrow for our children and our children's children.

PART ☆ TWO

Consumer Travelogue

COUNTRIES TABLE
AND COUNTRIES PAGES

This section of the book will examine a number of foreign countries that do trade with the United States by detailing the state of their manufacturing and what kind of import/export relationship we have with this country. It is intended to work as a practical guide for those who have read the book and become interested in how their purchases affect the world as well as the U.S. economy.

The type of detail includes information on each country's trade with the United States, which brands and products they export to us, what type of government they have, and if any American companies operate in their country. These details are presented with other relevant facts that give the reader a good overall idea of what buying, for example, a product that is "Made in Italy" really means to them, to the people making the product, and particularly to the United States economy. If a country has a particularly poor or a particularly good record of environmental protection or human rights measures, this is also noted.

We also present each country's trade balance with the United States as well as the trade ratio between their country and ours, using 2010 data. This information should give the reader a good overview of how purchases of products originating in these countries will affect the U.S. economy, as well as the economy and citizens of the foreign nation in question. To keep this book compact, the Travelogue details only the countries you are most likely to encounter on consumer product labels.

List of Sources Used in Travelogue

- Information for the country profiles is gathered from *The CIA World Fact-book 2010*, a reference resource produced by the Central Intelligence

Agency, which collects information from a number of American government agencies, as well as the U.S. State Department.

- The trade numbers are quoted from The United States Census Bureau 2010 statistics on foreign trade.

- Environmental performance is estimated using the *"2010* Environmental Performance Index" (or EPI), a research study compiled jointly by Yale University and Columbia University and commissioned by The World Economic Forum in Davos, Switzerland and presented at the annual World Economic Forum in 2010. The index ranks 163 countries across ten policy categories, measuring how close countries are to established environmental policy goals.

- Information on worker rights was drawn principally from the annual reports of the U.S. State Department, Bureau of Democracy, Human Rights, and Labor: 2010 Country Reports on Human Rights Practices www.state.gov/j/drl/rls/hrrpt/2010/index.htm, April 8, 2011.

- Human Rights information comes from Freedom House, an independent international non-governmental (NGO) and watchdog organization based in Washington, D.C., and their report "Freedom in the World 2011." Transparency International's "2010 World Corruption Index" report is also used for this category.

- Tourism and travel information is provided by the United States Department of Commerce's Office of Travel and Tourism Industries, and their latest report, "2009 United States Resident Travel Abroad."

- Product information comes from the websites of the companies listed, as well as transnationale.org.

Additional sources include:

- Peter Stalker: *Oxford Guide to the Countries in the World* (Oxford University Press, 2010)

- *Press Freedom Index 2010* by Reporters Without Borders

- Other additional sources are quoted where appropriate.

Trade Statistics Information for Countries Trading with the United States

Country	Trade Ratio with U.S.	Trade Balance ($ millions)	Exports to U.S. as % of total Exports	Imports from U.S. as % of total Imports	GDP per capita adjusted for PPP¤
Afghanistan*	25.27	2070.2	14.9	29.1	$900
Albania	1.97	14.3	1.9	1.0	$8,000
Algeria*	0.08	-13323.3	24.9	3.1	$7,300
Andorra	15.40	7.2	0.8	0.5	$46,700
Angola*	0.11	-10646	23.0	9.0	$8,200
Antigua & Barbuda	28.78	152.8	8.0	25.0	$16,400
Argentina*	1.94	3592.4	5.4	13.8	$14,700
Armenia	1.50	37.9	8.2	3.5	$5,700
Australia*	2.54	13214.7	4.0	11.1	$41,000
Austria*	0.36	-4407.6	4.0	1.4	$40,400
Azerbaijan	0.13	-1735.9	8.4	3.7	$10,900
The Bahamas	3.94	2371.1	35.9	23.6	$28,700
Bahrain	2.97	829.3	2.9	12.2	$40,300
Bangladesh*	0.13	-3716.3	22.1	2.7	$1,700
Barbados	9.29	354.6	8.8	24.7	$21,800
Belarus	0.76	-41.4	0.7	0.4	$13,600
Belgium*	1.64	9904.1	5.3	5.3	$37,800
Belize	2.41	169	30.3	34.0	$8,400
Benin	1544.67	463.1	0.0	7.2	$1,500
Bhutan	8.75	3.1	0.1	0.4	$5,500
Bolivia	0.75	-172.8	12.3	11.9	$4,800
Bosnia & Herzegovina	1.03	0.8	0.5	0.3	$6,600
Botswana	0.29	-121.2	0.0	3.5	$14,000
Brazil*	1.48	11467.2	9.6	15.0	$10,800
Brunei	10.44	112.3	0.1	4.4	$51,600
Bulgaria	0.66	-88.8	1.3	0.7	$13,500
Burkina Faso	19.42	44.2	0.2	2.9	$1,200

*Asterisks before country indicate that there is a full page about the country in this travelogue.

Country	Trade Ratio with U.S.	Trade Balance ($ millions)	Exports to U.S. as % of total Exports	Imports from U.S. as % of total Imports	GDP per capita adjusted for PPP¤
Burma	N/A	9.7	0.0	0.2	$1,400
Burundi	4.24	11	4.2	2.9	$300
Cambodia	0.07	-2147	47.3	2.6	$2,100
Cameroon	0.45	-164.8	6.4	2.7	$2,300
Canada*	0.90	-28542.5	74.9	50.0	$39,400
Cape Verde	7.14	8.6	1.4	1.3	$3,800
Central African Republic	1.81	4.6	3.5	3.3	$700
Chad	0.04	-1955.9	71.9	8.1	$1,600
Chile*	1.56	3896.1	10.0	17.0	$15,400
China*	0.25	-273063.3	18.0	7.3	$7,600
Colombia*	0.77	-3590	42.0	25.5	$9,800
Congo-Kinshasa	0.18	-434.3	10.4	1.8	$300
Congo-Brazzaville	0.08	-3061.7	31.1	8.0	$4,100
Costa Rica*	0.60	-3517.5	33.6	40.1	$11,300
Côte d'Ivoire (Ivory Coast)	0.14	-1013.9	10.2	2.4	$1,800
Croatia	0.94	-21.4	2.7	1.5	$17,400
Cuba	1226.33	367.6	0.0	4.1	$9,900
Cyprus	12.11	123.3	0.4	1.6	$21,000
Czech Republic	0.58	-1039.4	1.9	1.1	$25,600
Denmark*	0.35	-3878.5	5.9	2.4	$36,600
Djibouti	40.93	119.8	4.3	5.0	$2,800
Dominica	45.50	71.2	3.7	13.4	$10,400
Dominican Republic*	1.79	2907.6	52.0	44.0	$8,900
Ecuador*	0.73	-2041.2	37.3	29.6	$7,800
Egypt*	3.05	4596.9	7.6	11.8	$6,200
El Salvador	1.10	227.4	43.5	32.1	$7,200
Equatorial Guinea	0.12	-1941.4	24.3	12.7	$36,600

Country	Trade Ratio with U.S.	Trade Balance ($ millions)	Exports to U.S. as % of total Exports	Imports from U.S. as % of total Imports	GDP per capita adjusted for PPP¤
Eritrea	24.00	2.3	0.5	0.3	$600
Estonia	0.27	-509.6	6.0	1.5	$19,100
Ethiopia	6.05	645.3	6.8	9.5	$1,000
Fiji	0.25	-135.1	15.7	3.4	$4,400
Finland*	0.56	-1702.1	5.5	3.4	$35,400
France*	0.70	-11386	5.1	4.6	$33,100
Gabon	0.11	-1969	30.4	9.9	$14,500
The Gambia	9.45	26.2	4.5	8.8	$1,900
Georgia	1.52	103.3	9.8	5.9	$4,900
Germany*	0.58	-34268.4	6.7	4.2	$35,700
Ghana	3.62	715.9	5.6	8.4	$2,500
Greece	1.39	310.2	3.8	2.4	$29,600
Grenada	9.26	63.6	11.0	18.8	$10,200
Guatemala*	1.40	1285.3	36.8	34.6	$5,200
Guinea	1.24	16.6	5.2	6.1	$1,000
Guinea-Bissau	3.78	2.5	0.7	1.6	$1,100
Guyana	0.97	-8.2	24.6	23.1	$7,200
Haiti	2.20	658.4	90.2	51.0	$1,200
Honduras*	1.17	674.1	65.0	50.7	$4,200
Hungary	0.52	-1199.8	2.7	1.5	$18,800
Iceland	1.61	123.7	4.5	8.9	$38,300
India*	0.65	-10282.5	12.6	5.7	$3,500
Indonesia*	0.42	-9532.2	9.1	6.9	$4,200
Iran	2.20	113.7	0.1	0.4	$10,600
Iraq*	0.14	-10501.3	24.3	6.6	$3,800
Ireland*	0.21	-26572	22.1	13.8	$37,300
Israel*	0.54	-9688	32.1	12.8	$29,800
Italy*	0.50	-14285.8	5.8	3.0	$30,500

Country	Trade Ratio with U.S.	Trade Balance ($ millions)	Exports to U.S. as % of total Exports	Imports from U.S. as % of total Imports	GDP per capita adjusted for PPP¤
Jamaica	5.07	1334	34.0	32.6	$8,300
Japan*	0.50	-60059.6	15.7	9.9	$34,000
Jordan	1.21	200.1	15.6	5.6	$5,400
Kazakhstan	0.39	-1142.1	3.1	2.3	$12,700
Kenya	1.21	64.3	5.8	3.5	$1,600
Korea, North	N/A	1.9	0.0	0.1	$1,800
Korea, South*	0.79	-10028.9	10.2	10.1	$30,000
Kosovo	112.00	11.1	0.0	0.4	$6,600
Kuwait	0.52	-2607.9	8.4	14.2	$48,900
Kyrgyzstan	20.36	75.5	0.2	2.4	$2,200
Laos	0.20	-47.1	3.0	0.7	$2,500
Latvia	1.79	151.7	2.1	3.3	$14,700
Lebanon	23.94	1924.9	1.5	10.4	$14,400
Lesotho	0.04	-287.6	58.4	4.4	$1,700
Liberia	1.06	11.4	18.1	26.3	$500
Libya	0.31	-1451.3	4.5	2.7	$14,000
Liechtenstein	0.14	-183.3	7.5	1.3	$141,100
Lithuania	0.99	-9.5	3.1	2.8	$16,000
Luxembourg	3.19	988.4	2.8	6.8	$82,600
Macedonia	0.91	-3.4	1.1	0.6	$9,700
Madagascar	1.07	7.6	9.2	4.3	$900
Malawi	0.52	-34.7	6.3	2.2	$800
Malaysia*	0.54	-11820.5	9.5	10.7	$14,700
Maldives	17.69	26.7	1.0	2.9	$6,900
Mali	5.92	31	0.2	1.3	$1,200
Malta	1.75	195.6	5.7	10.3	$25,600
Marshall Islands	7.73	79.4	60.8	31.6	$2,500
Mauritania	1.58	30.5	2.6	4.2	$2,100

Country	Trade Ratio with U.S.	Trade Balance ($ millions)	Exports to U.S. as % of total Exports	Imports from U.S. as % of total Imports	GDP per capita adjusted for PPP¤
Mauritius	0.20	-156.4	11.0	1.0	$14,000
Mexico*	0.71	-66434.9	73.5	60.6	$13,900
Micronesia	10.12	38.3	30.0	18.5	$2,200
Moldova	3.02	25.3	0.8	1.0	$2,500
Monaco	2.01	24.7	3.4	1.8	$30,000
Mongolia	9.96	103.9	0.4	3.5	$3,600
Montenegro	3.74	10.7	7.6	7.5	$10,100
Morocco	2.84	1261.6	4.2	6.2	$4,800
Mozambique	3.47	159.7	2.4	4.7	$1,000
Namibia	0.57	-84	4.8	0.0	$6,900
Nauru	12.50	2.3	n/a	3.5	$5,000
Nepal	0.47	-32.2	7.5	0.5	$1,200
Netherlands*	1.83	15884.3	4.0	6.8	$40,300
New Zealand*	1.02	56.8	8.6	10.5	$27,700
Nicaragua	0.49	-1026.2	58.2	23.4	$3,000
Niger	1.85	22.4	12.2	2.6	$700
Nigeria*	0.13	-26448.2	37.4	9.3	$2,500
Norway*	0.45	-3851.3	5.0	5.4	$54,600
Oman	1.43	331.7	2.2	5.5	$25,600
Pakistan*	0.54	-1607.5	15.8	4.9	$2,500
Palau	142.00	14.1	0.0	16.0	$8,100
Panama	15.91	5681.8	5.3	10.0	$13,000
Papua New Guinea	1.92	89.4	1.6	4.3	$2,500
Paraguay	29.15	1748	0.7	16.6	$5,200
Peru*	1.34	1697.4	16.1	24.7	$9,200
Philippines*	0.92	-605.9	13.4	9.9	$3,500
Poland*	1.01	18.7	1.8	1.8	$18,800
Portugal*	0.49	-1083.1	4.4	1.5	$23,000

Country	Trade Ratio with U.S.	Trade Balance ($ millions)	Exports to U.S. as % of total Exports	Imports from U.S. as % of total Imports	GDP per capita adjusted for PPP¤
Qatar	6.77	2693.3	0.8	15.5	$179,000
Romania	0.72	-277.9	1.9	1.2	$11,600
Russia*	0.23	-19684.6	5.6	2.4	$15,900
Rwanda	1.42	9.1	5.3	2.7	$1,100
Saint Kitts & Nevis	2.59	80.4	56.5	39.5	$13,700
Saint Lucia	22.56	383.7	17.2	11.4	$11,200
Saint Vincent & the Grenadines	47.78	84.2	3.2	14.5	$10,300
Samoa	5.79	15.8	13.1	4.6	$5,500
San Marino	1.05	0.2	0.2	0.4	$36,200
São Tomé & Príncipe	4.67	1.1	2.2	1.4	$1,800
Saudi Arabia*	0.37	-19856.5	13.0	12.4	$24,200
Senegal	42.82	213.3	0.2	4.9	$1,900
Serbia	0.63	-60.1	1.7	0.6	$10,900
Seychelles	1.65	4.2	1.5	1.2	$23,200
Sierra Leone	2.11	32.1	9.0	6.6	$900
Singapore	1.67	11590.2	6.5	11.5	$62,100
Slovakia	0.24	-817.1	1.6	0.4	$22,000
Slovenia	0.71	-137	1.9	1.3	$28,200
Solomon Islands	5.00	4	0.5	2.3	$2,900
Somalia	15.00	1.4	0.1	0.2	$600
South Africa*	0.69	-2589	10.1	7.0	$10,700
Spain*	1.19	1624.9	3.4	3.2	$29,400
Sri Lanka*	0.10	-1569.6	19.6	1.5	$5,000
Sudan	14.27	107.5	0.1	1.3	$2,300
Suriname	1.89	170.5	13.0	26.6	$9,700
Swaziland	0.20	-97.4	6.9	1.2	$4,500
Sweden*	0.45	-5788.6	6.4	3.2	$39,100

Country	Trade Ratio with U.S.	Trade Balance ($ millions)	Exports to U.S. as % of total Exports	Imports from U.S. as % of total Imports	GDP per capita adjusted for PPP¤
Switzerland*	1.08	1542.2	10.2	5.3	$42,600
Syria	1.17	73.8	3.6	3.3	$4,800
Taiwan*	0.73	-9802.6	11.5	10.0	$35,700
Tajikistan	38.00	55.5	0.1	1.9	$2,000
Tanzania	3.82	120.7	1.1	2.4	$1,400
Thailand*	0.40	-13716.2	10.4	5.9	$8,700
Togo	17.40	149.2	1.1	6.1	$900
Tonga	11.50	18.9	17.9	10.8	$6,100
Trinidad & Tobago*	0.29	-4687.3	44.2	27.8	$21,200
Tunisia	1.41	165.1	2.4	0.0	$9,400
Turkey*	2.51	6338.6	3.5	6.6	$12,300
Turkmenistan	0.83	-8.3	0.5	0.5	$7,500
Uganda	1.62	35.8	1.9	2.2	$1,300
Ukraine	1.26	280.8	2.1	2.2	$6,700
United Arab Emirates*	10.19	10528	0.6	7.7	$49,600
United Kingdom*	0.97	-1361.5	11.4	5.8	$34,800
Uruguay	4.14	739.6	3.5	8.3	$13,700
Uzbekistan	1.48	33	0.6	1.3	$3,100
Vanuatu	11.81	17.3	4.0	5.2	$5,100
Venezuela*	0.33	-22058	38.7	26.6	$12,700
Vietnam*	0.25	-11158.9	20.0	4.6	$3,100
Yemen	2.15	209.5	2.4	4.7	$2,700
Zambia	1.91	26.8	0.4	1.2	$1,500
Zimbabwe	1.15	8.7	2.3	1.7	$500

¤GDP for each country is presented in Purchasing Power Parity (PPP) terms. PPP evens out differences in cost of living, so that we can compare economic conditions in nations with drastic price differences more accurately.

*Country listed in Travelogue.

Chart made with data from U.S Census Bureau's Foreign Trade Statistics and *CIA World Factbook 2011*.

AFGHANISTAN   TRADE RATIO: 25.36

U.S. TRADE BALANCE WITH AFGHANISTAN
Surplus of $2 billion
Exports to Afghanistan: $2.2 billion
Imports to U.S.: $0.08 billion

Government Type: Islamic Republic
Population: 29 million
Unemployment: 35%

AFGHANISTAN'S MAIN TRADE PARTNERS
Exports: Pakistan 25.9%,
          India 25.5%, USA 14.9%
Imports: USA 29.1%, Pakistan 23.3%,
          India 7.6%
Economy: Services 42.1%,
          Agriculture 31.6%,
          Industry 26.3%

How important is American consumerism to the country?
Afghanistan is not a major exporter of consumer goods. That said, the United States is the third largest export destination for goods originating from the country. Exports consist mostly of agricultural products.

Products from Afghanistan (*Company of local origin)
Carpets, wool, cotton, fruits and nuts, opium, gems

Did you know?
About half the government's budget comes from international aid due to troubled infrastructure.

Human rights
Afghanistan gets very low marks from Freedom House for their citizens' freedoms. Fraudulent elections in 2010 lowered the marks even more. Citizens' rights are routinely repressed and civil liberties are denied. Instability caused by the Taliban's resurgence has made it difficult for the government to gain full control of the nation, leaving their citizens vulnerable.

Environment
EPI does not list Afghanistan among its countries, as the country does not have reliable data on its environment due to its unstable governmental situation. However, continuing war and heavy use of natural resources has taken its toll on the country's environment.

Tourism
There are no available records kept of how many U.S. tourists visit Afghanistan.

ALGERIA
TRADE RATIO: 0.08

U.S. TRADE BALANCE WITH ALGERIA
Deficit of: $13.3 billion
Exports to Algeria: $1.2 billion
Imports to U.S.: $14.5 billion

Government Type: Republic
Population: 35 million
Unemployment: 10%

ALGERIA'S MAIN TRADE PARTNERS
Exports: USA 22.9%, Italy 12.6%, Spain 11.9%
Imports: France 15.1%, China 11.6%, Italy 9.1%
Economy: Industry 61.6%, Services 30.1%, Agriculture 8.3%

How important is American consumerism to the country?
97% of Algeria's exports consist of petroleum and natural gas, 17% of that going to the United States. Only very small amounts of anything else are exported to America. This includes cocoa and some fruits—but consumer goods are a negligible amount of the deficit with Algeria.

Products from Algeria (*Company of local origin)
Oil, natural gas, cocoa, fruit

Did you know?
About 80% of Algeria is covered by the Sahara desert.
Philosopher Albert Camus hailed from Algeria.

Human rights
Human rights have been an issue in Algeria, with press freedom and freedom of speech limited by the government, corruption having been an issue and rigged elections suspected—leading to Algerians participating in mass protests in late 2010 and spring 2011 which promised broader rights for their citizens in the future.

Environment
Algeria ranks highest among all African or Middle Eastern countries in the EPI comparison, ranking 42nd in the world. Water scarcity problems and air pollution are cited as the main problems, but they are well placed in comparison with similar countries.

Tourism
Due to the civil war, there were only 33 American tourists recorded as visitors to Algeria in 2009.

ANGOLA

TRADE RATIO: 0.11

U.S. TRADE BALANCE WITH ANGOLA

Deficit of $10.6 billion
Exports to Angola: $1.3 billion
Imports to U.S.: $11.9 billion

Government Type: Republic
Population: 13 million
Unemployment: not available

ANGOLA'S MAIN TRADE PARTNERS

Exports: China 37%, USA 24.5%,
India 8.7%
Imports: Portugal 19.7%,
China 15.1%, USA 9%
Economy: Industry 65.8%,
Services 24.6%,
Agriculture 9.6%

How important is American consumerism to the country?

Angola mostly exports oil to the United States—next to no consumer goods. This may change in the future, as Angola rebuilds its agriculture and diamond industries following three decades of devastating civil war. Coffee especially may become an export in the future, though the plantations suffered greatly in the war.

Products from Angola (*Company of local origin)

Oil

Did you know?

Angola is one of the world's poorest countries and its life expectancy is one of the lowest in Africa at under 40 years.

Angola was a Portuguese colony until its independence in 1975.

Angola is the seventh largest country in Africa, about twice the size of Texas.

Human rights

Three decades of civil war have left the country in a state of disrepair. Oil income could have made it a rich nation had it not been torn apart by war, which finally ended in 2002. Press freedom has been gradually improving but civil liberties are still weak, as are political rights.

Environment

Only three countries get worse scores for their environment than Angola in the EPI study. This may obviously be a result of the civil war having crippled decision-making for an extended period.

Tourism

There are no available records kept of how many U.S. tourists visit Angola.

ARGENTINA

TRADE RATIO: 1.95

U.S. TRADE BALANCE WITH ARGENTINA

Surplus of $3.6 billion
Exports to Argentina: $7.4 billion
Imports to U.S.: $3.8 billion

Government Type: Republic
Population: 41 million
Unemployment: 7.9%

ARGENTINA'S MAIN TRADE PARTNERS

Exports: Brazil 20.5%, Chile 7.9%, USA 6.6%
Imports: Brazil 31.1%, USA 13.3%, China 12.4%
Economy: Services 59.8%, Industry 31.6%, Agriculture 8.5%

How important is American consumerism to the country?
The U.S. is the third biggest export market for Argentina, responsible for about 6.5% of their exports. Much of these exports are industrial products, including oil and aluminum, but there are also consumer goods including beef, fruits, and vegetables.

Products from Argentina (*Company of local origin)
Soybeans, oil, corn, wheat, fruit, beverages, *Malbec* wine

Did you know?
The word "Argentina" means "land of silver."
Argentina is the eighth largest country in the world.
Argentina is the world's sixth largest wine-producing country.[1]

Human rights
There have been some concerns over human rights in Argentina, but for the most part it is a free country where its citizens have human rights that are respected. There have been some incidents limiting press freedom, but the country is still well above average on that respect as well. However, corruption has been a major issue and remains widespread.

Environment
Argentina ranks almost exactly in the middle of the EPI ranking. Of concern are the state of their fisheries (are they being depleted?) and major air pollution, as well as relatively high greenhouse gas emissions.

Tourism
Nearly 400,000 Americans visit Argentina annually, enough to rank it 26th in the list of Americans' most popular travel destinations.

AUSTRALIA   TRADE RATIO: 2.54

U.S. TRADE BALANCE WITH AUSTRALIA	AUSTRALIA'S MAIN TRADE PARTNERS
Surplus of $13.2 billion	*Exports:* China 21.8%, Japan 19.2%, South Korea 7.9%
Exports to Australia: $21.8 billion	*Imports:* China 17.9%, USA 11.3%, Japan 8.4%
Imports to U.S.: $8.6 billion	*Economy:* Services 70.5%, Industry 21.1%, Agriculture 3.6%
Government Type: Constitutional monarchy	
Population: 21.7 million	
Unemployment: 5.2%	

How important is American consumerism to the country
U.S. is the fifth largest export partner for Australia, accounting for just under 5% of their total exports. China is by far their biggest export destination.

*Products from Australia (*Company of local origin)*
*Billabong**
Minerals, coal, iron, gold, aluminum, natural gas

Did you know?
Australia has dedicated the most land area to organic farming in the world.[2] It is also the world's second biggest producer of gold.[3]
The world's largest reef, The Great Barrier Reef, is located in Australia. It is larger in size than the country of England.

Human rights
No human rights issues to report.

Environment
Australia has a fairly strong, certainly above average approach to environmental issues. They come in 51st in the EPI test, certainly not near the top, but well ahead of the United States and Canada, perhaps due to a strong response to the threat of climate change and an eroding farm land.

Tourism
636,000 Americans visited Australia in 2009, enough for it to be the 18th most popular tourist destination for Americans.

AUSTRIA

TRADE RATIO: 0.33

U.S. TRADE BALANCE WITH AUSTRIA

Deficit of $4.4 billion
Exports to Austria: $2.4 billion
Imports to U.S.: $6.8 billion

Government Type: Republic
Population: 8.2 million
Unemployment: 4.4%

AUSTRIA'S MAIN TRADE PARTNERS

Exports: Germany 31%, Italy 8.2%, Switzerland 5%
Imports: Germany 45.1%, Switzerland 6.8%, Italy 6.7%
Economy: Services 69.4%, Industry 27.5%, Agriculture 5.5%

How important is American consumerism to the country?
The U.S. is not a major trade partner with Austria, with its share making up about 3.5% of all exports.

Products from Austria (*Company of local origin)
Red Bull*, Glock*
Machinery, paper and paper products, motor vehicles and their parts, textiles, foodstuffs, metal, iron and steel goods, chemicals

Did you know?
Austria is among the most forested nations in Europe—more than half of its land is covered in forest.
Pez candy was invented in Austria.

Human rights
No reported human rights issues.

Environment
Austria is among the European leaders in environmental protection, ranking 8th in the world in the EPI country comparison. Over sixty percent of Austria's energy is supplied by renewable resources.

Tourism
About 400,000 Americans visit Austria per year. It is the 25th most popular travel destination for Americans.

BANGLADESH

TRADE RATIO: 0.13

U.S. TRADE BALANCE WITH BANGLADESH

Deficit of $3.7 billion
Exports to Bangladesh: $0.6 billion
Imports to U.S.: $4.3 billion
Government Type: Republic
Population: 158 million
Unemployment: 5.1% (but over 40% are severely underemployed)

BANGLADESH'S MAIN TRADE PARTNERS

Exports: USA 22.1%, Germany 14.1%, United Kingdom 8.5%
Imports: China 18.9%, India 12.7%, Singapore 6%
Economy: Services 52.6%, Industry 28.5%, Agriculture 18.8%

How important is American consumerism to the country?

Over 20% of Bangladesh's exports reach American shores—most of them consumer goods such as apparel and food.

Products from Bangladesh (*Company of local origin)

Garments and apparel, leather and leather goods, jute products, fish and seafood (particularly frozen fish).

Levi Strauss has 15 sub-contractors in Bangladesh supplying them with goods.[4] Many major apparel companies have a manufacturing presence in Bangladesh, including *H&M, Nike, Reebok, J.C Penney* and *The Gap*.[5]

Did you know?

Bangladesh is the world's second largest producer of jute.

Human rights

About 40% of the population lives below the poverty line. Poverty has consequences for health of the population as well; half of Bangladesh's children are malnourished, and adult literacy is just over 50%. In 2010 the country nearly doubled its official minimum wage in the garment industry, which had previously been extremely low. The State Department notes that child labor and abuse of children remain a problem, particularly in the informal sector. The legal rights of freedom of association and collective bargaining are rarely protected in practice. Labor organizers report frequent acts of intimidation and abuse, arbitrary lock-outs and firings, as well as increased scrutiny by security forces. Garment factories are commonly forced to work overtime, experience delay in their pay, and are denied full-leave benefits.

Environment

Bangladesh gets a poor mark in the EPI. There is a large amount of pollution, fisheries are in decline and trawled extensively, causing unsustainable damage to the fisheries and there is little protection of fragile areas. Climate change is expected to hit Bangladesh hard, with annual flooding already a problem.

BELGIUM

TRADE RATIO: 1.63

U.S. TRADE BALANCE WITH BELGIUM
Surplus of $9.9 billion
Exports to Belgium: $25.5 billion
Imports to U.S.: $15.5 billion
Government Type: Constitutional monarchy
Population: 10.4 million
Unemployment: 8.3%

BELGIUM'S MAIN TRADE PARTNERS
Exports: Germany 19.6%, France 17.7%, Netherlands 11.8%
Imports: Netherlands 17.9%, Germany 17.1%, France 11.7%
Economy: Services 73%, Industry 25%, Agriculture 2%

How important is American consumerism to the country?
America is Belgium's fifth largest trading partner. Most of their exports go to the European Union. A large proportion of Belgium's manufacturing companies are also foreign-owned, including some American-owned companies, such as a Ford plant employing nearly 5000 people there, making vehicles for the European market.[6]

Products from Belgium (*Company of local origin)
*Ecover**
Number 1 export to U.S. is pharmaceuticals, followed by chemicals.
Belgian chocolate is their tastiest export.

Did you know?
75% of Belgium's trade is with other European nations.
Belgium is the world's largest producer of azaleas.
In 2011 Belgium broke the world record, previously held by Iraq, for the longest wait without a government, at 249 days, when the squabbling parties were not able to agree on a coalition to run the country.[7]

Environment
Belgium's environmental record is ranked by EPI as worse than most Central European countries. It scores on that particular index about the same as Jamaica and the Ukraine, an unimpressive showing for a Western European country. Belgium has very little protected forest area, and the largest area devoted to buildings per person in the EU—showing conservation is not a priority in the country. Belgium gets over half of their energy needs from nuclear power.

Tourism
257,000 Americans visited Belgium in 2009.

BRAZIL

TRADE RATIO: 1.48

U.S. TRADE BALANCE WITH BRAZIL

Surplus of $11.5 billion
Exports to Brazil: $35.4 billion
Imports to U.S.: $23.9 billion

Government Type: Republic
Population: 203 million
Unemployment: 6.7%

BRAZIL'S MAIN TRADE PARTNERS

Exports: China 12.5%, USA 10.5%,
Argentina 8.4%
Imports: USA 16.1%, China 12.6%,
Argentina 8.8%
Economy: Services 67.4%,
Industry 26.8%,
Agriculture 5.8%

How important is American consumerism to the country?
10% of exports go to the United States—mostly agricultural products. Meanwhile their top imports include electrical equipment, machinery and vehicles.

Products from Brazil (*Company of local origin)
Top exports to U.S. include meat, sugar, tea and coffee, although the number one export is oil. Foreign companies with plants there: *Cargill* (cooking oils, mayo, salad dressing), *PepsiCo (Cheetos, Gatorade, Quaker), Nestlé* (coffee, mineral water, desserts with chocolate), *Nabisco, Kellogg* and many more.

Did you know?
Brazil is South America's leading producer of milk, meat and eggs. It is also the world's second largest producer of ethanol fuels.[8]
Total U.S. trade with Brazil has more than doubled since 2003.
Brazil is the largest country in South America and the fifth largest country in the world, behind Russia, Canada, China, and the United States. Brazil now has the eighth largest economy in the world.

Environment
Destruction of Brazil's rainforests is a major loss for the entire world. Each year 1.5% to 4% of Brazil's forests are destroyed for logging purposes.

Tourism
667,000 visitors from America traveled to Brazil in 2009. It is the 19th most visited destination from the United States.

CANADA

TRADE RATIO: 0.90

U.S. TRADE BALANCE WITH CANADA	CANADA'S MAIN TRADE PARTNERS
Deficit of $28.5 billion	*Exports:* USA 75.1%, United Kingdom 2.7%, China 2.2%
Exports to Canada: $249 billion	*Imports:* USA 51.1%, China 10.9%, Mexico 4.6%
Imports to U.S.: $277 billion	*Economy:* Services 71.5%, Industry 26.3%, Agriculture 2.2%
Government Type: Constitutional monarchy	
Population: 34 million	
Unemployment: 8%	

How important is American consumerism to the country?

Canada is our second largest trade partner by volume. A vast majority of Canadian exports—75%—go to the United States. Without oil products, there is actually a small surplus for the United States in manufactured goods trade.

Products from Canada (*Company of local origin)

Blackberry*, Lululemon*, Molson* (Includes *Coors, Miller, Blue Moon, Carling* etc.), *Labatt*, Sleeman*, Seagram Whisky*, EuroCom**—computers/laptops, *Bombardier**—snowmobiles, ohvs etc., *Electrolux**—stoves, etc.

Did you know?

Canada is America's largest source of oil imports.

Canada is the world's second largest producer of hydroelectricity and the largest producer of flax seeds in the world, most of which are exported.

Canada is a crucial market for many U.S. companies. It is the leading export destination for 35 of the 50 states and is a larger market for U.S. goods than all 27 countries of the European Union put together.[9]

Environment

The EPI ranks Canada 46th in the world in achieving its environmental policy goals. Its environmental reputation and scores in various rankings tend to be hurt by Canada's aggressive oil exploration and their exploitation of the Tar Sands in Alberta for oil, causing pollution and extremely high carbon emissions.

Tourism

Close to twelve million Americans visit Canada each year. Due to its close proximity and shared border, it is the second most popular destination for foreign travel for Americans.[10]

CHILE

TRADE RATIO: 1.56

U.S. TRADE BALANCE WITH CHILE

Surplus of $3.8 billion
Exports to Chile: $10.9 billion
Imports to U.S.: $7.1 billion

Government Type: Republic
Population: 16.9 million
Unemployment: 7.1%

CHILE'S MAIN TRADE PARTNERS

Exports: China 23.2%, USA 11.2%, Japan 9.2%
Imports: USA 16.8%, China 11.8%, Argentina 10.9%
Economy: Services 53.1%, Industry 41.8%, Agriculture 5.1%

How important is American consumerism to the country?

The United States is the second largest export destination for Chilean goods after China, with an 11% share of all goods leaving their borders. This includes consumer goods like food, wine, paper and pharmaceuticals, as well as industrial use goods like minerals and chemicals.

Products from Chile (*Company of local origin)

Food products, berries and fruits, wine, *Goodyear* tires[11], *Adidas* and *Nike* apparel, pharmaceuticals, paper

Did you know?

80% of Chile is covered by mountains.
40% of the population lives in the area in or near the capital Santiago.
Chile has two of the world's largest copper mines.
Easter Island belongs to Chile and is a major tourist attraction.
Chile is a world leader in copper mining.

Human rights

No major issues reported.

Environment

Chile ranks second behind Colombia in all South American countries and 16th worldwide in the EPI ranking, between notable environmental performers New Zealand and Germany, which speaks for their good record.

Tourism

According to the Department of State, about 160,000 Americans visit Chile annually.

CHINA

TRADE RATIO: 0.25

U.S. TRADE BALANCE WITH CHINA	CHINA'S MAIN TRADE PARTNERS
Deficit of $273 billion	*Exports:* USA 18.4%, Hong Kong 13.8%, Japan 8.2%
Exports to China: $91 billion	*Imports:* Japan 13%, South Korea 10.2%, USA 7.7%
Imports to U.S.: $364 billion	*Economy:* Industry 46.9%, Services 43%, Agriculture 10.2%
Government Type: Single-party communist republic	
Population: 1.3 billion	
Unemployment: 4.3% (urban only)	

How important is American consumerism to the country?
18% of China's exports go to the United States, making up a huge dollar value in their trade surplus.

Products from China (*Company of local origin)
Nearly all consumer product categories include things made, harvested or assembled in China. About 20% of all imports to America come from China. To give some scale of how large a category this is, nearly 70% of all goods for sale at Wal-Mart are of Chinese origin.[12]

Did you know?
China is the world's top food producer, as well as the largest manufacturer of goods, having overtaken the United States in output. However, China needs 100 million workers to produce slightly more than the United States does with 11.5 million people.

Human rights
Multiple human rights violations. One-party republic, limited political and civil rights and freedom of speech. According to the U. S. State Department's Country reports on Human Rights Practices, censorship is common; there is no federal minimum wage, and no effective right to strike. There is child labor, forced labor (including prison labor), and persecution of political dissent.

Environment
China is the world's largest emitter of CO_2. The European Union estimated that only 1% of Chinese people living in cities are breathing air that is safe and clean.[13] China is investing heavily in renewable energy technologies and is the world leader in solar panel production for instance.

Tourism
Around 1.2 million American residents traveled to China in both 2009 and in 2010, making it the 9th most popular travel destination for people from the United States.

COLOMBIA

TRADE RATIO: 0.77

U.S. TRADE BALANCE WITH COLOMBIA:
DEFICIT OF $3.6 BILLION
Exports to Colombia: $12.1 billion
Imports to U.S.: $15.7 billion

Government Type: Republic
Population: 44.7 million
Unemployment: 11.8%

COLOMBIA'S MAIN TRADE PARTNERS
Exports: USA 42%, EU 12.6%,
China 5.2%
Imports: USA 25.5%, China 13.4%,
Italy 9.4%
Economy: Services 53.1%,
Industry 37.6%,
Agriculture 9.2%

How important is American consumerism to the country?
The U.S. is the largest export market for Colombia, accounting for a huge 42% of all exports. The biggest export item is oil, followed by coffee, coal, minerals, apparel, and fruit.

Products from Colombia (*Company of local origin)
70% of imports is made up of petroleum products, followed by gold.
Flowers, coffee, fruit, plastics and apparel are also imported.
Products from *Chiquita, Adidas, Levi Strauss* and *Nike* are also exported to the U.S.

Did you know?
Colombia supplies the world with a large portion of its emeralds, gold, silver and platinum. The capital city of Bogotá lies at 8,200 feet.

Human rights
Colombia is characterized by Freedom House as "partly free." Despite some progress, the State Department reports that labor rights are frequently abridged and do not apply to workers in associated workers' cooperatives (CTAs). The campaign of violence against trade unionists continues; 51 deaths were reported in 2010. Child labor and forced labor are not uncommon. NGOs report that as any as 2 million children work, and nearly forty percent of them receive no payment. Drug trade still runs rampant in Colombia, but corruption has been reduced in recent years. Press freedom is also a concern in Colombia, where two journalists were murdered in 2010.

Environment
Colombia ranks 10th in the world and 1st among South American nations in the EPI ranking, showing their excellent environmental record. Colombia made heavy investments into hydroelectric energy, reducing their emissions per unit of energy produced and they have an excellent record in forest conservation.

Tourism
545,000 Americans visited Colombia in 2009, ranking it 22nd among Americans' most popular destinations, just ahead of Switzerland.

COSTA RICA

TRADE RATIO: 0.60

U.S. TRADE BALANCE WITH COSTA RICA:	COSTA RICA'S MAIN TRADE PARTNERS:
Deficit of $3.5 billion *Exports to Costa Rica:* $5.2 billion *Imports to U.S.:* $8.7 billion *Government Type:* Republic *Population:* 4.6 million *Unemployment:* 7.3%	*Exports:* USA 35.9%, China 8.8%, Netherlands 6.8% *Imports:* USA 42.1%, Mexico 6.5%, China 6.2% *Economy:* Services 71%, Industry 22.5%, Agriculture 6.5%

How important is American consumerism to the country?

Nearly 36% of all Costa Rican exports end up in the United States, by far the largest export market for them. Exports are mostly consumer goods such as food items and electronic equipment.

Products from Costa Rica (*Company of local origin)

Bananas, coffee, pineapples, watermelons, sugar, flowers, seafood, beef; *Acer, Motorola* and *Intel* electronics, pharmaceuticals, apparel including *Levi Strauss, Fruit of the Loom* and *Reebok, Bridgestone Tires.*[14]

Did you know?

Costa Rica was the first nation in the world to abolish its military. It has not had a standing army since 1949.

Costa Rica has officially targeted being the world's first carbon-neutral country by the start of the next decade.

About a quarter of the country's land area is either national park land, or conservation area.

Human rights

No issues, a healthy democracy.

Environment

Costa Rica is a model country when it comes to their environmental policies, having made it a national priority. A large proportion of the land area is protected and its rainforests are not being logged at a significant rate. They rank 3rd in the world in the EPI environmental ranking.

Tourism

It is estimated that more than 700,000 Americans visit Costa Rica annually. According to the Department of State, it is also home to about half a million American citizens, many of them retirees.

DENMARK

TRADE RATIO: 0.35

U.S. TRADE BALANCE WITH DENMARK

Deficit of $3.9 billion
Exports to Denmark: $2.1 billion
Imports to U.S.: $6 billion
Government Type: Constitutional monarchy
Population: 5.5 million
Unemployment: 5.9%

DENMARK'S MAIN TRADE PARTNERS

Exports: Germany 17.5%, Sweden 12.8%, United Kingdom 8.5%
Imports: Germany 21%, Sweden 13.1%, Norway 7%
Economy: Services 76.6%, Industry 22.1%, Agriculture 1.2%

How important is American consumerism to the country?
The U.S. is the fourth largest export market for Denmark, receiving about 6% of their exports.

Products from Denmark (*Company of local origin)
LEGO*, Arla Foods*, Carlsberg*
Exports also include pharmaceuticals, machinery, windmills, meat, dairy, and fish products.

Did you know?
Denmark earns more than 3% of its national income from producing clean technologies—more than any other country in the world. They are particularly advanced in wind power technology.
Greenland and the Faroe Islands belong to Denmark.

Human rights
Advanced

Environment
Denmark is a leader in renewable energy production, as visitors witness from the dozens of windmills at seemingly every town along its highways. Some reports claim Denmark produces over a fifth of its energy needs with wind power.[15] However, Denmark's fisheries are stressed and it remains a high greenhouse gas emitting nation, bringing forth concerns about its environmental policies.

Tourism
More than 300,000 Americans visit Denmark annually.

DOMINICAN REPUBLIC

TRADE RATIO: 1.79

U.S. TRADE BALANCE WITH DOMINICAN REP.:
Surplus of $2.9 billion
Exports to D.R: $6.6 billion
Imports to U.S.: $3.7 billion

Government Type: Republic
Population: 10 million
Unemployment: 13.3%

D.R.'S MAIN TRADE PARTNERS
Exports: USA 53.4%, Haiti 9.7%,
Imports: USA 44.3%, Venezuela 6%,
China 5%

Economy: Services 64.6%,
Industry 28.3%,
Agriculture 7.1%

How important is American consumerism to the country
A massive 53% of exports end up in the United States, making it by far their most important trade partner.

Products from the Dominican Republic (*Company of local origin)
Coffee, sugar, silver, gold, cocoa, tobacco, consumer goods, apparel including products by *Nabisco, Nestlé, Avon Cosmetics, Colgate, Palmolive, Gillette, Microsoft,* plus many apparel companies including *Levi Strauss, Liz Claiborne, Nike, Quicksilver, The Gap, Reebok* and *Victoria's Secret.*

Did you know?
Dominican Republic has the largest market share in organically grown banana exports.[16]
A major export for the country to the United States is professional baseball players. Opening day in MLB in 2011 featured 86 players born in the baseball-mad Dominican Republic, where many clubs have founded "academies" for spotting young talent.[17]

Human rights
Human rights are generally respected in Dominican Republic, where its citizens enjoy relatively high levels of freedom. The World Bank calls it a "lower-middle-income developing country."

Environment
Dominican Republic fared quite well in the 2010 Environmental Performance Index, being ranked 36th in the world in their environmental policies. This is in stark contrast to Haiti, the neighboring country they share their island with, who, in a very similar natural environment, are in 155th place. This indicates that the Dominican Republic is keeping their environment healthy, and especially their forest conservation efforts are considered successful.

Tourism
A large number of Americans vacation in the Dominican Republic. In 2010 it was visited by 1.8 million Americans, making it the 4th most popular tourist destination for people from the U.S.

ECUADOR

TRADE RATIO: 0.73

U.S. TRADE BALANCE WITH ECUADOR

Deficit of $2 billion
Exports to Ecuador: $5.4 billion
Imports to U.S.: $7.5 billion
Government Type: Republic
Population: 15 million
Unemployment: 7.6%

ECUADOR'S MAIN TRADE PARTNERS

Exports: USA 33.6%, Panama 14.3%, Peru 6.8%
Imports: USA 25.4%, Colombia 10.6%, China 7.2%
Economy: Services 57.7%, Industry 35.9%, Agriculture 6.4%

How important is American consumerism to the country?
One-third of all exports go to the United States, making it by some distance the largest export market for Ecuador. 65% of that is made up by petroleum, but the remainder includes consumer goods, mostly foodstuffs and plants.

Products from Ecuador (*Company of local origin)
Dole, Nabisco, Nestlé, Xerox, Nike, Kia Motors

Did you know?
Ecuador is the world's top banana exporter, accounting for a whopping one-third of all international banana exports.
Ecuador is the leading exporter of fresh fruit in the world, tied with Spain.

Human rights
Ecuador is considered "partly free" by Freedom House's report. Press freedom is somewhat limited because of violence and intimidation towards journalists. Ecuador also ranks poorly in the corruption comparison, coming in towards the bottom of Latin American countries in that index.

Environment
Ecuador rounds up the top 5 of Latin American territories in the EPI comparison, and has a score only a bit behind that of Spain. Their fisheries and water systems are in good order and agriculture is in sustainable shape. The problems are mostly centered around pollution and high greenhouse emissions, but overall, Ecuador shows a good environmental record.

Tourism
About 250,000 Americans visit Ecuador each year.

EGYPT

TRADE RATIO: 3.05

U.S. TRADE BALANCE WITH EGYPT
Surplus of $4.6 billion
Exports to Egypt: $6.8 billion
Imports to U.S.: $2.2 billion

Government Type: Republic
Population: 82 million
Unemployment: 9%

EGYPT'S MAIN TRADE PARTNERS
Exports: Spain 6.8%, Italy 6.7%, USA 6.3%
Imports: USA 10.6%, China 8.7%, Germany 8%
Economy: Services 48.3%, Industry 37.5%, Agriculture 14%

How important is American consumerism to the country?
United States is Egypt's third largest export partner with about 6% of their exports coming to the U.S. Apparel, textiles, and carpets make up a healthy proportion of that share. Egypt also exports some oil to the U.S.

Products from Egypt (*Company of local origin)
Food products: *Heinz, Danone, Nestlé, Cadbury,* fruit & vegetables
Electrolux, Philips, Xerox, Michelin, Pirelli
Pharmaceuticals, apparel, clothing, textiles, carpets

Did you know?
Egypt is Africa's second most populous country after Nigeria.
95% of the population lives on just 5% of the territory, along the Nile River.

Human rights
Autocratic regime of Hosni Mubarak was overthrown by a wave of protests in early 2011, a new government was still being formed at the time of this writing, but human rights improvements were expected.

Environment
Egypt is scored slightly above average for its region as well as its income group, but still comes in only ranked 68th in the EPI comparison (although that places them only a few spots below the United States). Air pollution and water concerns are the most pressing environmental problems for Egypt.

Tourism
About 275,000 visitors from America head to Egypt each year. It ranks 32nd on the list of most popular destinations for American visitors.

FINLAND

TRADE RATIO: 0.56

U.S. TRADE BALANCE WITH FINLAND
Deficit of $1.7 billion
Exports to Finland: $2.2 billion
Imports to U.S.: $3.9 billion

Government Type: Republic
Population: 5.3 million
Unemployment: 8.4%

FINLAND'S MAIN TRADE PARTNERS
Exports: Germany 10.3%, Sweden 9.8%, Russia 8.9%
Imports: Russia 16.2%, Germany 15.8%, Sweden 14.7%
Economy: Services 68.1%, Industry 29%, Agriculture: 2.9%

How important is American consumerism to the country?
The United States is the fourth most important export nation for Finland, with about 8% of their exports ending up in America. Cruise ships and paper products make up the bulk of the exports.

Products from Finland (*Company of local origin)
Nokia*, Arabia* (dishware), Marimekko* (fabrics), Iittala* (kitchenware), Finn-Crisps*, Wasa* (food products) Suunto*, Fiskars*

Did you know?
A quarter of Finland's territory lies north of the Arctic Circle.
Finland has more than 180,000 lakes.
There are 1.8 million saunas in Finland—enough for approximately one for every three Finns.
Finland is the most sparsely populated country in the European Union.

Human rights
No issues

Environment
Finland ranks 12th in the world Yale EPI comparison out of 163 countries. Finland creates nearly 30% of its electricity with nuclear power plants[18] and an impressive 15% from hydropower—however, much of the remainder is coal and petroleum-based.

Tourism
Finland was visited by around 85,000 Americans in 2009.

FRANCE

TRADE RATIO: 0.70

U.S. TRADE BALANCE WITH FRANCE	FRANCE'S MAIN TRADE PARTNERS
Deficit of $11.3 billion	*Exports:* Germany 15.9%, Italy 8.2%, Spain 7.8%
Exports to France: $27 billion	*Imports:* Germany 19.4%, Belgium 11.6%, Italy 8%
Imports to U.S.: $38.3 billion	
Government Type: France	*Economy:* Services 79.5%, Industry 18.5%, Agriculture 2%
Population: 65 million	
Unemployment: 9.3%	

How important is American consumerism to the country?
The United States was the 6th largest export destination of French goods in 2010, behind the largest European economies. Just about 5.65% of exports went to the United States.

Products from France (*Company of local origin)
Peugeot*, Renault,* Elysée*, L'Oréal*, Yves Rocher*, Louis Vuitton*, Michelin*, Orange*, Ubisoft Entertainment*, DailyMotion*, Chanel*, Christian Dior*, Hermés*, Jean Paul Gaultier*, Lacoste*
Food and wine, champagne

Did you know?
With over 75 million tourists each year, France is the world's most visited country.

Human rights
Transparency International ranked France as the 25th least corrupt country in the world. Citizens enjoy widespread freedom and civil and political liberties, although Freedom House has expressed some concern over spreading discrimination against ethnic minorities in the country.

Environment
France gets high scores for its environmental approach, ranking seventh in the world in the Environmental Performance Index.

Tourism
1.9 million Americans visited France in 2009, making France along with Italy and Germany the 5th most popular countries for American tourism, and the second most popular in Europe behind Great Britain.

GERMANY

TRADE RATIO: 0.58

U.S. TRADE BALANCE WITH GERMANY

Deficit of $34.3 billion
Exports to Germany: $48.2 billion
Imports to U.S.: $82.4 billion

Government Type: Republic
Population: 81 million
Unemployment: 7.1%

GERMANY'S MAIN TRADE PARTNERS

Exports: France 10.1%, USA 6.7%, United Kingdom 6.6%
Imports: Netherlands 13%, France 8.2%, Belgium 7.2%
Economy: Services 71.3%, Industry 27.8%, Agriculture 0.9%

How important is American consumerism to the country?

America is the second largest export destination for Germany, although with only a 6.7% share. If treating the EU as a single entity, it is by far the most important market for German companies. Indeed, France is the number 1 export destination with 10% of German exports going to their western neighbors.

Products from Germany (*Company of local origin)

Mercedes-Benz*, BMW*, Audi*, Porsche*, Mini*, Volkswagen*, Siemens*, Bosch*, Carl Zeiss*, Bauer*, Bertelsmann*, Continental Tires*, Adidas*, Puma*, Esprit Europe*, Hugo Boss*, Stihl*

Did you know?

Germany is the world's second largest exporter, behind China, in spite of its relatively small population of a little over 80 million people.
Germany is located in heart of Central Europe, and shares a border with nine countries. The approximately 80 million people in Germany live in a land approximately the size of Montana.

Environment

EPI ranks Germany 17th in environmental policy. The green party has exceptionally high support and influence in Germany. They are also a major industry leader in renewable energies, especially solar power.

Tourism

With over 1.5 million visitors yearly, Germany ranks with France and Italy as the 5th most visited nation in the world for travelers from the United States.

GUATEMALA

TRADE RATIO: 1.40

U.S. TRADE BALANCE WITH GUATEMALA
Surplus of $1.28 billion
Exports to Guatemala: $4.5 billion
Imports to U.S.: $3.2 billion

Government Type: Republic
Population: 13.8 million
Unemployment: 3.2%

GUATEMALA'S MAIN TRADE PARTNERS
Exports: USA 41.6%, El Salvador 9.3%, Honduras 7.9%
Imports: USA 37.1%, Mexico 11.3%, China 6.3%
Economy: Services 63%, Industry 23.8%, Agriculture 13.2%

How important is American consumerism to the country?
The United States is *the* most important market for Guatemalan goods, making up over 40% of all their exports.

Products from Guatemala (*Company of local origin)
Chiquita, Philip Morris, Colgate-Palmolive, L'Oréal, Xerox, Novartis, Hexal (pharmaceuticals), Goodyear, Del Monte, Nestlé, Dole
Apparel, coffee, fruit, sugar, bananas, cardamom, oil, cigarettes

Did you know?
Guatemala is the sixth largest producer of coffee in the world. Coffee makes up 32% of all its exports.[19]
Guatemala is also the leading producer of the spice cardamom, with 66% of world production.[20]

Human rights
Organized crime groups and criminal gangs are fairly powerful in Guatemala, and their law enforcement officials have been criticized by Human Rights Watch for being too weak and corrupt to help contain these groups. Violent crime is common. By law, all civilian workers have the right to form and join trade unions of their choice. Violence against unionists and worker activists combined with weak and ineffective enforcement of labor and employment laws restrict this right in practice, according to the State Department.

Environment
Guatemala ranks rather poorly in the EPI study, coming behind many of its Central American neighbors at 104th. Air pollution, loss of forest cover and lack of protection for critical habitats were primary factors that caused their poor showing.

Tourism
About 180,000 Americans visit Guatemala annually.

HONDURAS

TRADE RATIO: 1.17

U.S. TRADE BALANCE WITH HONDURAS

Surplus of $0.67 billion
Exports to Honduras: $4.6 billion
Imports to U.S.: $3.9 billion
Government Type: Republic
Population: 8.1 million
Unemployment: 5.1% (but 1/3 of population is underemployed)

HONDURAS' MAIN TRADE PARTNERS

Exports: USA 40.9%, El Salvador 8.6%, Guatemala 7.2%
Imports: USA 33.9%, Guatemala 10.5%, Mexico 6.8%
Economy: Services 60.9%, Industry 26.5%, Agriculture 12.5%
Percentage of population below poverty line: 65%

How important is American consumerism to the country?

The United States is the most important market for Honduran producers, with over 40% of products exported to the U.S.

Products from Honduras (*Company of local origin)

Most apparel companies, including *Wal-Mart, American Apparel, Fruit of the Loom, Levi's,* and *Nike*
Coffee, bananas, shrimp, wire harnesses, palm oil, fruit, lobster, cigars

Did you know?

Half of Honduras' economic activity is directly tied to the United States—exports to the U.S. account for 30% of their GDP.
Much of the ancient Mayan culture was located in what is now Honduras.

Human rights

Main concerns voiced by Human Rights Watch include continuing threats and violence against journalists, activists and others defending human rights as well as attacks on transgender people in particular.

Environment

Honduras ranks a poor 118th out of 163 nations involved in the EPI study. Loss of forest cover was a major issue cited in the data.

Tourism

Somewhere around 100,000 Americans visit Honduras each year.

HONG KONG

TRADE RATIO: 6.18

U.S. TRADE BALANCE WITH HONG KONG	HONG KONG'S MAIN TRADE PARTNERS
Surplus of $22.3 billion	*Exports:* China 52.7%, USA 11%, Japan 4.2%
Exports to Hong Kong: $26.5 billion	*Imports:* China 45.1%, Japan 9.6%, Taiwan 7.4%
Imports to U.S.: $4.3 billion	*Economy:* Services 92.5%, Industry 7.4%, Agriculture 0%
Government Type: Special administrative region of China	
Population: 7.1 million	
Unemployment: 4.4%	

How important is American consumerism to the country?
The USA receives 11% of their exports, the second largest export destination for Hong Kong's goods. Hong Kong's primary trade is in services, and not so much goods.

Products from Hong Kong (*Company of local origin)
Electronics, machinery, appliances, watches & clocks, textiles and apparel, toys, precious stones and jewelry

Did you know?
Hong Kong is home to one of the world's largest film industries. It is also a major publishing and broadcasting hub.
Hong Kong has the most skyscrapers in the world, with about 8,000, about twice as many as New York City.

Human rights
A mix of British elective tradition and Chinese customs and rule make it a more democratic area than other parts of China. Hong Kong is also an area with low corruption, although money laundering is frequent as it is an international financial and banking hub. Civil liberties are well respected. However, Freedom of Assembly is not possible and there is no formal labor law at all, sometimes resulting in many people working extremely long hours.

Tourism
Hong Kong received 788,000 American visitors in 2009, placing it as the 13th most popular destination for Americans.

INDIA

TRADE RATIO: 0.58

U.S. TRADE BALANCE WITH INDIA

Deficit of $10.3 billion
Exports to India: $19.3 billion
Imports to U.S.: $29.5 billion

Government Type: Republic
Population: 1.1 billion
Unemployment: 10.8%

INDIA'S MAIN TRADE PARTNERS

Exports: UAE 12.5%, USA 11.1%, China 6.1%

Imports: China 11.2%, USA 6.5%, UEA 6%

Economy: Services 55.5%, Industry 26.3%, Agriculture 18.5%

How important is American consumerism to the country?

The U.S. is India's second largest export destination, after the United Arab Emirates, with over an 11% share. India exports both raw materials for industry as well as consumer products like textiles.

Products from India (*Company of local origin)

Precious stones, apparel and textiles, electronics

Did you know?

India's Mumbai-based Bollywood film industry produces more movies each year than any other country.

Human rights

Human Rights Watch expresses some concern over discrimination against *Dalits* (or "the untouchables"), tribal groups and religious minorities, as well as forced land acquisition by the government which often leaves rural farmers displaced.

Environment

In the Environmental Performance Index, India ranks near the tail end at 123rd. Because of their lax environmental regulations, India has recently even become a destination for western companies to "export" their emissions by opening polluting plants there to get around tightening regulations in Europe and North America.

Tourism

Over a million people visit India from American each year. It is the 12th most visited nation from the United States.

INDONESIA

TRADE RATIO: 0.42

U.S. TRADE BALANCE WITH INDONESIA
DEFICIT OF $9.5 BILLION
Exports to Indonesia: $6.9 billion
Imports to U.S.: $16.5 billion

Government Type: Republic
Population: 245 million
Unemployment: 7.1%

INDONESIA'S MAIN TRADE PARTNERS
Exports: Japan 15.9%, China 9.9%, USA 9.3%
Imports: Singapore 16.1%, China 14.5%, Japan 10.2%
Economy: Industry 47%, Services 37.6%, Agriculture 15.3%

How important is American consumerism to the country?
The U.S is Indonesia's third largest export partner, accounting for 9.3% of all exports in 2009. A large percentage of exports are consumer goods, such as apparel, electronics, food and furniture.

Products from Indonesia (*Company of local origin)
Rubber, textiles, apparel including *Adidas, Levi's, Nike, Quicksilver, Reebok, The Gap*
Pharmaceuticals, plywood, wood and paper products
Electronics including *Sanyo, Pioneer, Thomson, NEC*

Did you know?
Indonesia is an archipelago consisting of 17,000 islands.

Human rights
Indonesia is characterized by Freedom House as a free country. It is noted for a relatively high level of corruption. Freedom of the press is also under threat, with several reporters receiving death threats for their reporting, and a pair of them having been killed in 2010 as well.

Environment
Indonesia receives poor marks for their environmental policies. High rates of logging by foreign and domestic companies deplete their forest cover. There is also severe air pollution.

Tourism
121,000 Americans visited in 2009, making it the 38th most visited nation in the world by Americans.

IRAQ

TRADE RATIO: 0.13

U.S. TRADE BALANCE WITH IRAQ
Deficit of $10.5 billion
Exports to Iraq: $1.6 billion
Imports to U.S.: $12.1 billion

Government Type: Republic
Population: 30 million
Unemployment: 15.3%

IRAQ'S MAIN TRADE PARTNERS
Exports: USA 25.2%, India 15.1%, South Korea 9.9%
Imports: Turkey 23.8%, Syria 16.6%, China 8.5%
Economy: Industry 60.5%, Services 27.3%, Agriculture 9.7%

How important is American consumerism to the country?
The U.S. is the fourth largest export market for Iraq. However, 99.9% of exports are petroleum and oil products.

Products from Iraq (*Company of local origin)
Oil makes up 85% of total exports and 99.9% of exports to the United States.

Did you know?
All U.S. troops withdrew from the country at the end of December 2011.
Iraq gained independence from the United Kingdom in 1932.
Sumer, in ancient Mesopotamia, now within the borders of Iraq, was one of the world's first civilizations.

Human rights
Improving, although corruption is a major problem in the wake of the U.S invasion and the rebuilding of the country's infrastructure nearly from scratch.

Environment
Iraq has no protected natural areas. Its water use is a concern to the EPI researchers; air pollution is problematic, as are diseases. It ranks well below average for its region in the study—obviously a result of a difficult governmental situation and different priorities for the previous regime.

Tourism
There are no available records of how many U.S. tourists visit Iraq.

IRELAND

TRADE RATIO: 0.21

U.S. TRADE BALANCE WITH IRELAND
Deficit of $26.5 billion
Exports to Ireland: $7.2 billion
Imports to U.S.: $33.8 billion

Government Type: Republic
Population: 4.6 million
Unemployment: 13.6%

IRELAND'S MAIN TRADE PARTNERS
Exports: USA 21%, Belgium 17%, United Kingdom 16.1%
Imports: United Kingdom 35.4%, USA 16.8%, Germany 6.8%
Economy: Services 70%, Industry 29%, Agriculture 2%

How important is American consumerism to the country?
The U.S. is the largest export destination of Irish goods, accounting for over 20% of all their exports.

Products from Ireland (*Company of local origin)
Software, electronics, pharmaceuticals, dairy (mainly cheese & butter), alcoholic beverages, etc.
Guinness*, *Hennessy's**, *Jameson's**
Foreign companies manufacturing in Ireland: *Microsoft* (Xbox games & software), *Hewlett Packard, IBM, Apple, Siemens, Google, Intel, Pfizer, Merck* [21], *Hasbro games*[22]

Did you know?
Ireland's economy is suffering in the wake of a massive economic implosion in 2008 caused by a property bubble. In 2010 the economy had to be bailed out with a $112 billion loan from the EU and the IMF. There are some 600 American subsidiaries in Ireland employing as many as 100 000 people.[23]
Ireland is one of the largest exporters of computer software in the world.
Google's European HQ is located in Dublin.
Ireland has one of the lowest corporate tax rates in the world at 12.5%, designed to attract foreign investment.
Tourism is a major industry, employing as much as 8% of the Irish workforce.

Environment
Ireland ranks 44th out of 163 countries in the Environmental Policy Index and 16 places above the United States and just below the European average in the 2010 rankings.

Tourism
About one million tourists from the United States and Canada visit Ireland each year[24]—the third largest origin country for tourists visiting Ireland. Total visitors to Ireland in 2008 numbered about 8 million.

ISRAEL

TRADE RATIO: 0.54

U.S. TRADE BALANCE WITH ISRAEL

Deficit of $9.7 billion
Exports to Israel: $11.3 billion
Imports to U.S.: $21billion

Government Type: Republic
Population: 7.5 million
Unemployment: 6.7%

ISRAEL'S MAIN TRADE PARTNERS

Exports: USA 35%, Hong Kong 6%, Belgium 5%
Imports: USA 12.3%, China 7.4%, Germany 7.1%

Economy: Services 65%, Industry 32.6%, Agriculture 2.4%

How important is American consumerism to the country?
The United States is by far the largest export destination for Israel, accounting for a sizable 35% of all exports, largely consumer goods.

Products from Israel (*Company of local origin)
Pharmaceuticals, apparel, *Timex* watches, salt
International companies with manufacturing in Israel: Food: *Danone, Nestlé, IFF* Electronics: *Intel, SanDisk, Broadcom, Texas Instruments, 3Com, Xerox, Hewlett Packard, Symantec*

Did you know?
Israel reuses 70% of its sewage and waste water, making it the world leader in recycled water use (by far—Spain is 2nd with just 12%).[25]

Human rights
Ongoing conflict between Israeli and Palestinian territories continues to do harm to both sides of the matter, and human rights, as in any conflict, have suffered.

Environment
Israel ranks in the middle of the pack in the EPI ranking. Their agricultural production is highlighted for its water-efficiency, a necessity because of their dry location.

Tourism
667,000 Americans visited Israel in 2009. It is the 15th most popular travel destination for U.S residents, and visitors from the United States are a major source of income for Israel's economy.

ITALY

TRADE RATIO: 0.50

U.S. TRADE BALANCE WITH ITALY	ITALY'S MAIN TRADE PARTNERS
Deficit of $14.3 billion	*Exports:* Germany 12.6%, France 11.6%, USA 5.9%
Exports to Italy: $14.2 billion	
Imports to U.S.: $28.5 billion	*Imports:* Germany 16.7%, France 8.9%, China 6.5%
Government Type: Republic	
Population: 61 million	*Economy:* Services 72.8%, Industry 25.3%, Agriculture 1.9%
Unemployment: 8.4%	

How important is American consumerism to the country?
Exports to the U.S. make up about 10% of Italy's total exports.

Products from Italy (*Company of local origin)
Food/wine, oils, pasta, etc.
High fashion: *Benetton, Dolce&Gabbana, Diesel, Versace, Armani, etc.*
Vehicles: *Ferrari, Lamborghini, Maserati, Fiat*

Did you know?
Italy produces more organic wine than any other country, and is fifth in the world in total area dedicated to organic farming.[26]
Italy is also the world's top producer of kiwi fruit.[27] Because the growing season for kiwis in Italy is opposite to that of other major producers, namely New Zealand, they have a market to export the furry fruit around the world to countries seeking a year-round supply, including the United States.

Human rights
Some corruption issues remain in the government, but overall there are no serious human rights concerns in Italy.

Environment
Italy ranks a strong 18th in the world in the EPI comparison, just behind northern neighbors Germany. Their environmental policies are slightly above European average.

Tourism
Nearly 2 million Americans visit Italy each year, ranking with France and Italy as the 5th most popular countries for American visitors.

JAPAN

TRADE RATIO: 0.50

U.S. TRADE BALANCE WITH JAPAN	JAPAN'S MAIN TRADE PARTNERS
Deficit of $60 billion	*Exports:* China 18.9%, USA 16.4%, South Korea 8.1%
Exports to Japan: $60.4 billion	*Imports:* China 22.2%, USA 11%, Australia 6.3%
Imports to U.S.: $120.5 billion	*Economy:* Services 73.8%, Industry 24.9%, Agriculture 1.4%
Government Type: Constitutional monarchy	
Population: 126 million	
Unemployment: 5%	

How important is American consumerism to the country?

16% of exports go to United States. Many American companies rely on high tech components like semiconductors and circuit boards from Japanese companies, which are industry leaders in many high tech fields. Japanese car manufacturers have a large slice of the American market, and have opened numerous factories in the United States as well, thereby also benefiting American workers.

Products from Japan (*Company of local origin)

Toyota*, Honda*, Mitsubishi*, Toshiba*, Panasonic*, Sony*, Fujitsu*, Nissan*, Yamaha*, Suzuki*, Subaru*, Asahi Breweries*, Canon*, Casio*, Kenwood*, Pioneer*, Sanyo*, Sharp*, Sony Ericsson*, Kawasaki*, NEC corp.*, Bridgestone Tires* (Including Firestone), Nintendo*, Sega Enterprises*, Nikon*, Ibanez* guitars, Konica*, Fujifilm*

Did you know?

Japan is the world's fifth largest exporter.
The Tokyo area with its 36 million inhabitants is the world's largest urbanized area.
The national sport of Japan is sumo wrestling.

Environment

Japan ranks twentieth in the world in the EPI study, the best placing for any Asian country, reflecting their good environmental credentials.

Tourism

Japan was ranked number 10 for the most popular destination for American tourists as 727,000 Americans visited Japan in the year 2010, by far the largest country of origin for tourists to Japan outside of Asia and fourth largest overall.

MALAYSIA

TRADE RATIO: 0.54

U.S. TRADE BALANCE WITH MALAYSIA	MALAYSIA'S MAIN TRADE PARTNERS
Deficit of $11.8 billion	*Exports:* Singapore 13.4%, China 12.6%, Japan 10.4%
Exports to Malaysia: $14.1 billion	*Imports:* China 12.6%, Japan 12.6%, Singapore 11.4%
Imports to U.S.: $25.9 billion	
Government Type: Constitutional monarchy	*Economy:* Services 48.2%, Industry 41.4%, Agriculture 10.5%
Population: 28.7 million	
Unemployment: 3.4%	

How important is American consumerism to the country?
United States is the 4th largest export destination for Malaysian goods, with a nearly 10% share of all their exports. It is also the biggest export destination outside of Asia, with China and Japan combining for the biggest share of about ¼ of all Malaysian exports.

Products from Malaysia (*Company of local origin)
Agricultural products, wood and paper products. Many foreign companies operate factories and assembly plants in Malaysia, including *Colgate, Palmolive, L'Oréal, Dow Chemical, DuPont, Cadbury, Campbell Soup, Nestlé, Danone, Procter & Gamble, Dyson, AMD, Intel, Pioneer, Thomson, Toshiba, Kenwood, Mattel, Bridgestone* and *Firewood* tires, *British American Tobacco, Adidas, Levi Strauss* and many other apparel companies.

Did you know?
Malaysia is one of the world's leading producers of palm oil, used widely in bio-diesels around the world. They are the world's top producer of certified sustainable palm oil, which makes up about 50% of all their palm oil production.
They are also among the world's top exporters of semiconductor devices, solar panels, ICT goods and electrical products.

Human rights
Malaysia's human rights scores are below average. The country is classified by Freedom House as "partly free", receiving a low score in both civil liberties and political freedoms. The same ruling party has been in power for decades, although elections do exist. There is some corruption as well, the country falling to 56th in the world in the Corruption Index.

Environment
Malaysia's environmental performance is a bit better than average. They finish ahead of nations like United States and Brazil in the EPI study.

Tourism
121,000 Americans visited Malaysia in 2009, making it the 38th most popular travel destination for Americans—resulting in considerable income for the Malaysian tourist and service industries.

MEXICO

TRADE RATIO: 0.71

U.S. TRADE BALANCE WITH MEXICO	MEXICO'S MAIN TRADE PARTNERS
Deficit of $66 billion	*Exports:* USA 80.6%, Canada 6%
Exports to Mexico: $163 billion	*Imports:* USA 48%, China 13.9%, Japan 4.9%
Imports to U.S.: $229 billion	
Government Type: Republic	*Economy:* Services 63.5%, Industry 32.6%, Agriculture 3.9%
Population: 113 million	
Unemployment: 5.4%	

How important is American consumerism to the country?

80% of Mexico's exports go to United States—their manufacturing industry and entire economy depends overwhelmingly on North America. Exports include automobiles, electrical equipment and appliances and other labor intensive manufactured goods that American and Canadian companies find cheaper to make in Mexico.

Products from Mexico (*Company of local origin)

Corn, sugar, various food products, fruits and vegetables, coffee, cotton, electrical equipment, alcoholic beverages, cars and vehicles

General Motors, Toyota, Bosch, Ford, Honda, Volkswagen, Gillette, Avon, Colgate, Revlon, Whirlpool, Electrolux, Acer, Bose, Canon, Casio, Intel, Fujitsu, Kenwood, Motorola, Philips, Pioneer, Sony, Thomson, Nokia, Ericsson, Dell, HP, Seagate, Symantec, Xerox, Hasbro, Mattel, IBM, Adidas, Christian Dior, Converse, Fruit of the Loom, Samsonite, The Gap, Nike, Bridgestone

Did you know?

Mexico is the world's largest silver producer.[28]
Mexico is the 2nd largest supplier of oil into the United States.

Human rights

Freedom House ranks Mexico as partly free. It receives an average 3 score in both civil liberties and political rights. Their score was downgraded in 2010 because of organized crime targeting officials and the government's inability to protect its citizens from criminal violence.

Environment

The EPI ranks Mexico 43rd, well ahead of the United States.

Tourism

In 2010, 20 million Americans visited Mexico and in 2008 the 20 million American tourists to Mexico spent $13.3 billion dollars when visiting. It is the most popular destination for foreign travel from the U.S. by a sizable margin.

THE NETHERLANDS

TRADE RATIO: 1.83

U.S. TRADE BALANCE WITH NETHERLANDS	THE NETHERLANDS'S MAIN TRADE PARTNERS
Surplus of $15.9 billion	*Exports:* Germany 25.8%, Belgium 12.6%, France 9.2%
Exports to Netherlands: $34.9 billion	*Imports:* Germany 16.8%, China 11.7%, Belgium 8.7%
Imports to U.S.: $19 billion	*Economy:* Services 72.5%, Industry 24.9%, Agriculture 2.6%
Government Type: Constitutional monarchy	
Population: 16.8 million	
Unemployment: 5.5%	

How important is American consumerism to the country?

The United States accounts for under 4% of Dutch exports. Most of their exports go to neighboring European nations, especially Germany.

Products from the Netherlands (*Company of local origin)

Philips*, Heineken*, Bols*, Shell*, Unilever* (owns Ben & Jerry's, Axe, Dove, Knorr, Lipton, Lux, Rexona, Sunsilk, and others)

Did you know?

The Netherlands is the world's largest exporter of fresh vegetables—including significant numbers exported to the United States.[29]
The Netherlands is the second biggest exporter in Europe after Germany.
A quarter of the Netherlands is below sea level.
There are twice as many bicycles as cars in the Netherlands.
The Netherlands is home to over a thousand museums.

Environment

As for environmental performance, the Netherlands trails most of their neighbors in central Europe and places 47 on the EPI ranking, just behind Canada.

Tourism

727,000 Americans visited the Netherlands in 2009, making it the 14th most popular destination for American tourists abroad.

NEW ZEALAND

TRADE RATIO: 1.02

U.S. TRADE BALANCE WITH NEW ZEALAND

Deficit of $13.3 billion
Exports to New Zealand: $2.8 billion
Imports to U.S: $2.7 billion
Government Type: Constitutional monarchy
Population: 4.3 million
Unemployment: 6.5%

NEW ZEALAND'S MAIN TRADE PARTNERS

Exports: Australia 23.4%, USA 9.6%, China 9.2%
Imports: Australia 18.4%, China 15.1%, USA 10.5%
Economy: Services 71%, Industry 24.3%, Agriculture 4.7%

How important is American consumerism to the country
The U.S. is the second most important export destination for goods from New Zealand, a large proportion of which goes directly to the consumer in the form of foodstuffs and consumer goods.

Products from New Zealand (*Company of local origin)
Meat, dairy, beverages, fish, wood products, fruits and nuts

Did you know?
Income from tourism makes up over 8% of the GDP.[30]
Exports make up 30% GDP, led by exports of dairy products.
About thirty percent of the land is covered by forest.
Bungee jumping originated in New Zealand.

Environment
New Zealand rounds out the top 15 of the EPI comparison, just behind the United Kingdom in the analysis of state environmental policy progress. Loss of biodiversity and high greenhouse emissions are pointed out as the only major issues in this regard in the study. A significant amount of New Zealand's energy is created from hydropower sources.

Tourism
333,000 Americans visited New Zealand in 2009, ranking it 29th on the list of most popular travel destinations from America.

NIGERIA   TRADE RATIO: 0.13

U.S. TRADE BALANCE WITH NIGERIA	NIGERIA'S MAIN TRADE PARTNERS
Deficit of $26.4 billion	*Exports:* USA 34%, India 9.8%, Brazil 9%
Exports to Nigeria: $4.1 billion	
Imports to U.S.: $30.5 billion	*Imports:* China 13.9%, USA 9.3%, Netherlands 8.6%
Government Type: Republic	*Economy:* Services 38%, Industry 32%, Agriculture 30%
Population: 155 million	
Unemployment: 4.9%	

How important is American consumerism to the country
About 96% of all Nigeria's exports to the United States are oil. Other exports include cocoa and rubber, which may be something American consumers may see on occasion, although it is often difficult to determine where those products come from.

Products from Nigeria (*Company of local origin)
Oil, cocoa, rubber, cotton

Did you know?
The Nigerian film industry dubbed "Nollywood" has become the second largest producer of films in the world.[31]
Nigeria is Africa's most populous country, and it is home to nearly one fifth of all the people in Africa.

Human rights
Nigeria suffers from high levels of corruption, from the top levels down, resulting in the state's high oil income not trickling down to its citizens. Two-thirds of the population lives beneath the poverty line. Education is also an issue, with only 68% of the population literate.

Environment
Nigeria's score in the EPI study is weaker than most other sub-Saharan African countries even, and it is in the bottom twenty in the study. Air pollution and water problems are among its biggest issues; a large quantity of Nigerians have limited or no access to sanitation or clean water.

Tourism
About 70,000 Americans visited Nigeria in 2009.

NORWAY

TRADE RATIO: 0.45

U.S. TRADE BALANCE WITH NORWAY

Deficit of $3.8 billion
Exports to Norway: $3.1 billion
Imports to U.S.: $6.9 billion

Government Type: Constitutional monarchy
Population: 4.7 million
Unemployment: 3.6%

NORWAY'S MAIN TRADE PARTNERS

Exports: United Kingdom 24.3%, Germany 13.4%, Netherlands 10.9%
Imports: Sweden 13.9%, Germany 12.9%, China 7.8%
Economy: Services 58.1%, Industry 39.4%, Agriculture 2.5%

How important is American consumerism to the country?

The United States are the 6th largest export market for Norway. About 45% of exports consist of oil. The rest is both consumer goods such as fish or electronics, industrial goods such as nickel and other minerals as well as machinery.

Products from Norway (*Company of local origin)

Fish, seafood, and boats

Did you know?

The world's longest road tunnel is located in Norway, over 15 miles long.
The petroleum sector provides nearly 30% of state income.
There are as many people of Norwegian descent in the United States as there are residents in Norway.
The cheese slicer was invented in Norway.

Environment

Norway is already preparing for their future without oil by making large scale investments into renewable energy sources and their development today. It ranks 5th in the world in the EPI study. Its score ranking is indicative of the forward-thinking environmental accomplishments in Norway.

Human rights

No recent issues.

Tourism

Norway was visited by around 114,000 Americans in 2009.

PAKISTAN

TRADE RATIO: 0.54

U.S. TRADE BALANCE WITH PAKISTAN	PAKISTAN'S MAIN TRADE PARTNERS
Deficit of $1.6 billion *Exports to Pakistan:* $1.9 billion *Imports to U.S.:* $3.5 billion *Government Type:* Republic *Population:* 187 million *Unemployment:* 15.4%	*Exports:* USA 15.8%, 　　Afghanistan 8.1%, UAE 7.9% *Imports:* China 17.9%, Saudi Arabia 　　10.7%, UAE 10.6% *Economy:* Services 54.6%, 　　Industry 23.6%, 　　Agriculture 21.8%

How important is American consumerism to the country?
The U.S. is the most significant trading partner for Pakistan, taking nearly 16% of their exports—almost all of that trade is in consumer goods.

Products from Pakistan (*Company of local origin)
Textiles, including clothing, linen, cloth and yarn, rice, leather goods, sports goods, manufactured goods, carpets and rugs, cotton
Levi Strauss lists 12 supplier factories in Pakistan.[32] *Adidas, Reebok and Nike* make soccer balls in Pakistan. Pakistan is the main source of soccer balls for the United States.[33]

Did you know?
The state of Pakistan was carved out of India in 1947 to create a new independent state for India's Muslim population.

Human rights
Poverty limits the human rights of Pakistani people in many ways. Over half of the adult population is illiterate. A third of the population lives below the poverty line and a third of children never enroll for primary education. The country has been striving to become more democratic in recent decades, but corruption is rampant, there is little stability in the political structures and recently Al-Qaeda terrorists have been attacking the country, further destabilizing it.

Environment
Pakistan ranks 125th in EPI, with about an average score for its income group. Severe air pollution, excessive deforestation and lack of environmental protections in general are issues the country faces—but with such an unstable government, it is hard to imagine it will tackle its environmental challenges in the near future.

Tourism
There were around 40,000 Americans who traveled to Pakistan in 2009.

PERU

TRADE RATIO: 1.34

U.S. TRADE BALANCE WITH PERU	PERU'S MAIN TRADE PARTNERS
SURPLUS OF $1.7 BILLION	*Exports:* USA 17.6%, China 15.3%, Switzerland 14.9%
Exports to Peru: $6.8 billion	*Imports:* USA 19.7%, China 15%, Brazil 7.6%
Imports to U.S.: $5.1 billion	
Government Type: Republic	*Economy:* Services 55%, Industry 35%, Agriculture 10%
Population: 29 million	
Unemployment: 7.9%	

How important is American consumerism to the country?
The U.S. is Peru's largest export partner with a 17% share. However, much of that is in oil, precious metals like gold and minerals like copper (61% of Peru's exports are mined). Consumer goods do account for some of that total, apparel, coffee and vegetables in particular, as well as pharmaceuticals.

Products from Peru (*Company of local origin)
Apparel: *Nike, The Gap, Levi Strauss, Reebok,* and *Goodyear*[34] all have factories in Peru.
Vegetables, coffee, fruit, fish, sugar

Did you know?
Peru is the world's second largest producer of silver and copper, and sixth largest gold producer.

Human rights
Freedom of press is limited, with censorship from the state and assaults on journalists somewhat common. Civil liberties of its people are, however, respected for the most part and citizens also enjoy political rights. Corruption is a problem, though not as common as in some other Latin American nations.

Environment
Peru ranks right behind Ecuador with a good showing in their environmental record in the Yale EPI ranking.

Tourism
About 428,000 Americans visited Peru in 2009, ranking it 24th on the list of most popular destinations for Americans.

PHILIPPINES

TRADE RATIO: 0.92

U.S. TRADE BALANCE WITH PHILIPPINES
Deficit of $0.6 billion
Exports to Philippines: $7.4 billion
Imports to U.S.: $8 billion

Government Type: Republic
Population: 102 million
Unemployment: 7.3%

PHILIPPINES'S MAIN TRADE PARTNERS
Exports: USA 17.7%, Japan 16.3%, Netherlands 9.5%
Imports: Japan 12.6%, USA 12%, China 8.9%
Economy: Services 54.8%, Industry 31.3%, Agriculture 13.9%

How important is American consumerism to the country?
The U.S. is the largest export market for Philippines, with a 17.7% share of their exports. This includes industrial materials, like minerals such as copper, as well as finished consumer goods like electronics and garments.

Products from Philippines (*Company of local origin)
Coconut oil, fruit and vegetables, fish and seafood
Apparel including from *Adidas, H&M, Levi's, Nike, Reebok, Hi-Tec Sports*
Electronics include *HP, NCR, NEC, 3Com, Intel, Toshiba, Texas Instruments*

Did you know?
The Philippines consists of over 7000 islands, lying between the China Sea and the Pacific Ocean.

Human rights
The Philippines had issues with corruption in the past that continue today, although 2010's election was commended by Freedom House as legitimate and transparent. However, press freedom is not guaranteed and civil liberties are not entirely complete in The Philippines.

Environment
The Philippines scores above the average for countries of its income group and well above the average of other countries in the Asian Pacific region. The main problems concern air pollution and loss of forest cover due to logging.

Tourism
394,000 Americans visited the Philippines in 2009, making it the 25th most popular country for American visitors.

POLAND

TRADE RATIO: 1.00

U.S. TRADE BALANCE WITH POLAND	POLAND'S MAIN TRADE PARTNERS
Surplus of $0.02 billion *Exports to Poland:* $3 billion *Imports to U.S.:* $3 billion *Government Type:* Republic *Population:* 38 million *Unemployment:* 12.1%	*Exports:* Germany 26.9%, France 7.1%, United Kingdom 6.4% *Imports:* Germany 29.1%, Russia 8.8%, Netherlands 6% *Economy:* Services 63.5%, Industry 33%, Agriculture 3.4%

How important is American consumerism to the country?

Less than two percent of Poland's exports go to the United States. A major part of those exports are consumer goods of all kinds.

Products from Poland (*Company of local origin)

Furniture, electronics, food products, manufactured goods, food, chemicals

Did you know?

Poland is a major producer of coal.

The private sector's share of GDP grew from 18% in 1989 to 88% in 2006, after the fall of the Soviet Union.

Poland is the 9th largest country in Europe.

Novelist Joseph Conrad, who wrote *Heart of Darkness*, was Polish, and in spite of writing in English always spoke with a strong Polish accent.

Human rights

Poland has a solid human rights record in recent history and is a free country.

Environment

Poland ranks 63rd, just behind the United States in the 2010 EPI study, scoring generally good marks in the examined categories. Air pollution and high emissions of greenhouse gases by industry are cited in the study as main environmental issues.

Tourism

Nearly 25,000 travelers from the United States visit Poland every year. It is tied with Singapore as the 35th most popular travel destination for American residents.

PORTUGAL

TRADE RATIO: 0.49

U.S. TRADE BALANCE WITH PORTUGAL
Deficit of $1 billion

Exports to Portugal: $1.1 billion

Imports to U.S.: $2.1 billion

Government Type: Republic
Population: 10.7 million
Unemployment: 10.8%

PORTUGAL'S MAIN TRADE PARTNERS
Exports: Spain 27.3%, Germany 12.9%, France 12.4%

Imports: Spain 32.6%, Germany 13.2%, France 8.3%

Economy: Services 74.7%, Industry 22.9%, Agriculture 2.4%

How important is American consumerism to the country
Only about 3.5% of Portugal's exports end up in the United States. About a third of that is petroleum.

Products from Portugal (*Company of local origin)
Corks (for wine bottles), apparel, textiles, beverages (port, wine)

Did you know?
Cork oak forests cover about 28% of Portugal's forests.[35]
Portugal produces about half the world's output of commercial cork.
The country receives about 16 percent of its foreign trade income from cork exports—as such, the country is waging "war" on the screw-top wine business.
About 20,000 Americans live in Portugal.

Environment
Portugal comes in just ahead of Japan, ranked 19th out of 163 nations in Yale University's EPI. In 2010, Portugal was reported to have generated a huge 45% of its energy needs using renewable energies, according to the *New York Times*.[36]

Tourism
171,000 people from the United States visited Portugal in 2009.

RUSSIA

TRADE RATIO: 0.23

U.S. TRADE BALANCE WITH RUSSIA
Deficit of $19.7 billion
Exports to Russia: $6 billion
Imports to U.S.: $25.7 billion

Government Type: Republic
Population: 139 million
Unemployment: 7.6%

RUSSIA'S MAIN TRADE PARTNERS
Exports: Netherlands 12.3%, Italy 7.1%, China 5.6%
Imports: China 14.2%, Germany 13.2%, Ukraine 5.6%
Economy: Services 59.1%, Industry 36.8%, Agriculture 4%

How important is American consumerism to the country?
The U.S. is not one of Russia's major export destinations. An overwhelming majority of Russia's exports to the United States are for industrial use, including petroleum and oil, as well as minerals—especially aluminum and iron.

Products from Russia (*Company of local origin)
Mostly raw materials, but consumers may see many alcoholic beverages imported from Russia at the liquor store—liquor is a major export for the country.

Did you know?
Russia is the world's top producer of gas, second in oil production, and fifth in coal. It is also the top producer of nickel, second in platinum and third in diamonds. Their wealth is clearly tied to their natural resources.

Human rights
Freedom House describes Russia as "not free." Political rights and civil liberties are both somewhat limited. Freedom of the press is weak, with dissenting journalists often having to escape the country for fear of violence. Russia is also ranked as one of the world's most corrupt nations by Transparency International's report.

Environment
Russia ranks 69th in the world in the EPI study, a bit above the average position. They lose marks mainly for severe air pollution issues and high greenhouse emissions.

Tourism
Russia receives about 300,000 visitors from America each year.

SAUDI ARABIA

TRADE RATIO: 0.37

U.S. TRADE BALANCE WITH SAUDI ARABIA
Deficit of $19.9 billion
Exports to Saudi Arabia: $11.6 billion
Imports to U.S.: $31.4 billion
Government Type: Constitutional monarchy
Population: 26 million
Unemployment: 10.8 %
(estimate for males only)

SAUDI ARABIA'S MAIN TRADE PARTNERS
Exports: Japan 15.4%, China 12.5%, USA 12.3%
Imports: USA 12.8%, China 10.6%, Germany 8.1%
Economy: Industry 61.8%, Services 35.7%, Agriculture 2.6%

How important is American consumerism to the country?
United States is the third largest export destination, with 12% of Saudi Arabia's exports heading here. Oil makes up 90% of their export earnings.

Products from Saudi Arabia (*Company of local origin)
Oil

Did you know?
Saudi Arabia is the largest country in the Middle East.
95% of its land mass is covered by desert.
Saudi Arabia is the world's largest producer of desalinated water.
Saudi Arabia is the second largest oil producer in the world behind Russia, supplying about 11% of the world's oil.

Human rights
Saudi Arabia is categorized as "not free" by Freedom House. Only men have the right to vote and civil liberties are weak—for instance, women are not allowed to drive. However, in 2005 there were open elections for the first time on town councils. All citizens are also entitled to free education and health care, and less wealthy citizens are entitled to a free plot of land.

Environment
Saudi Arabia is not noted for its conservation initiatives, perhaps because it sits on 20% of the world's known oil reserves. It is ranked 99th in the world on Yale University's EPI.

Tourism
86,000 people from the United States visited Saudi Arabia in 2009.

SINGAPORE

TRADE RATIO: 1.66

U.S. TRADE BALANCE WITH SINGAPORE

Surplus of $11.6 billion
Exports to Singapore: $29 billion
Imports to U.S.: $17.4 billion

Government Type: Republic
Population: 4.7 million
Unemployment: 2.2%

SINGAPORE'S MAIN TRADE PARTNERS

Exports: Hong Kong 11.6%, Malaysia 11.5%, China 9.8%
Imports: USA 11.9%, Malaysia 11.6%, China 10.6%
Economy: Services 71.7%, Industry 28.3%, Agriculture 0%

How important is American consumerism to the country?

The U.S. is the fifth largest export destination for Singapore, and the largest outside of Asia, accounting for 6.6% of all of their exports. Consumer goods are a large export category of Singapore, so American consumers contribute to their economy in a significant way.

Products from Singapore (*Company of local origin)

Electronics (circuit boards and their hi-tech parts): *Compaq, Dell, HP, Seagate, AMD, Broadcom, Canon, Kenwood, Nvidia, Motorola, Sony, Toshiba, Thomson, Texas Instruments*

Did you know?

Singapore has the highest proportion of millionaires to its population anywhere in the world, with more than 15% of its households having more than $1 million in assets.

Human rights

There some issues since Singapore is controlled by an autocratic government. The ruling party often sues political opponents for defamation, resulting in their bankruptcy which makes them ineligible to stand for parliament. Freedom of the press is limited, citizens are often held without trial, and citizen's right to privacy is reportedly infringed upon in some instances.

Singapore is, however, a country virtually free of corruption. It ties for first place in the world with Denmark and New Zealand in Transparency International's ranking with an exceptionally high score of 9.3 out of 10.

Environment

Singapore also has a relatively high ranking in the EPI score, coming in 28th in the world. Only Japan, among Asian countries, did better in the comparison.

Tourism

242,000 visitors from America visited Singapore in 2009.

SOUTH AFRICA

TRADE RATIO: 0.69

U.S. TRADE BALANCE WITH SOUTH AFRICA	SOUTH AFRICA'S MAIN TRADE PARTNERS
Deficit of $2.6 billion *Exports to South Africa:* $5.6 billion *Imports to U.S.:* $8.2 billion *Government Type:* Republic *Population:* 49 million *Unemployment:* 24.9%	*Exports:* China 10.3%, USA 9.2%, Japan 7.6% *Imports:* China 17.2%, Germany 11.2%, USA 7.4% *Economy:* Services 66.7%, Industry 30.8%, Agriculture 2.5%

How important is American consumerism to the country?
The United States is the second largest export market for South Africa, with a share of just under 10% of all their exports. Exports include machinery and electronics, foodstuffs including fruit, as well as diamonds and other metals.

Products from South Africa (*Company of local origin)
Diamonds, food: *Dole, Del Monte, Nestlé, McCain, Procter & Gamble, L'Oréal, Dell, Symantec, Xerox*

Did you know?
South Africa is a world leader in gold and diamond output.
There are 11 official languages recognized by the government.

Human rights
Although current president Jacob Zuma was suspected of corruption around the time of his election in 2008, Transparency International ranks South Africa as a country with fairly low corruption—especially for a sub-Saharan African nation.
A massive 18% of the population is infected with HIV/AIDS, and access to health programs for some groups is limited; inequalities remain rampant two decades after the fall of Apartheid. Half the population lives below the poverty line.

Environment
South Africa ranks towards the bottom in the EPI study, 115th out of 163 countries.

Tourism
273,000 visitors from America headed to South Africa in 2009, ranking it 32nd on the list of most popular visitor destinations.

SOUTH KOREA
TRADE RATIO: 0.79

U.S. TRADE BALANCE WITH SOUTH KOREA	SOUTH KOREA'S MAIN TRADE PARTNERS
Deficit of $10 billion	*Exports:* China 23.9%, USA 10.4%, Japan 6%
Exports to South Korea: $38.8 billion	*Imports:* China 16.8%, Japan 15.3%, USA 9%
Imports to U.S.: $48.9 billion	*Economy:* Services 58.2%, Industry 39.3%, Agriculture 2.6%
Government Type: Republic	
Population: 49 million	
Unemployment: 3.7%	

How important is American consumerism to the country?
The United States is the second largest export market for South Korea with over 10% of exports coming to the U.S. The biggest imports from South Korea to the United States include electronic equipment (including computers and parts like semiconductors), machinery and vehicles.

Products from South Korea (*Company of local origin)
Samsung*, LG*, Daewoo*, Hyundai*, Kia*, Adidas, Hermés, Levi's, Nike, Reebok, Samsonite, Continental Ag, Lego, 3Com

Did you know?
South Korea makes about 50% of the world's LCD screens.
Daewoo Motor is owned by General Motors.
Nearly 40,000 U.S troops continue to be stationed in South Korea.

Human Rights
No reported issues.

Environment
South Korea is ranked especially low, at 94th in the Environmental Performance Index, one of the lowest rankings for a high-income nation in the study. Air pollution, lack of conservation efforts, high greenhouse emissions and the state of their fisheries were areas of concern in the Yale University comparison.

Tourism
667,000 visitors from America chose South Korea as their destination in 2009.

SPAIN

TRADE RATIO: 1.19

U.S. TRADE BALANCE WITH SPAIN	SPAIN'S MAIN TRADE PARTNERS
Surplus of $1.6 billion	*Exports:* France 19.5%, Germany 11.4%, Portugal 9.2%
Exports to Spain: $10.2 billion	*Imports:* Germany 14%, France 12.8%, Italy 7.4%
Imports to U.S.: $8.6 billion	*Economy:* Services 70.7%, Industry 26%, Agriculture 3.3%
Government Type: Constitutional monarchy	
Population: 46 million	
Unemployment: 20.1%	

How important is American consumerism to the country?

The United States is not among the top 5 export partners for Spain, accounting for only about 3.5% of all exports. A vast majority of exports go elsewhere in the European Union.

Products from Spain (*Company of local origin)

Exports include machinery, pharmaceuticals, food—especially fruits, vegetables and wine, consumer goods and motor vehicles.

Did you know?

Together with Ecuador, Spain is the world's leading exporter of fresh fruit. In 2010, Spain recorded a trade deficit of $63 billion—only Italy and the United States did worse that year.

Human rights

Spain is a free country with all the Western European rights and freedoms for its people. For instance, gay marriage is legal. Spain is also a country with relatively low corruption and strong press freedom.

Environment

Spain ranks 25th in the world in the EPI comparison. They have a number of progressive energy policies, for instance, getting a large proportion of their electricity from wind and solar sources. Still, the EPI find fault with the amount of protected ecosystems and natural habitats, as well as high carbon emissions.

Tourism

Over a million Americans visit Spain every year, making it the 11th most visited destination for Americans.

SRI LANKA

TRADE RATIO: 0.10

U.S. TRADE BALANCE WITH SRI LANKA

Deficit of $1.6 billion
Exports to Sri Lanka: $0.2 billion
Imports to U.S.: $1.8 billion

Government Type: Republic
Population: 21 million
Unemployment: 5.8%

SRI LANKA'S MAIN TRADE PARTNERS

Exports: USA 20.5%, United Kingdom 12.8%, Italy 5.5%
Imports: India 17.5%, China 15.9%, Singapore 7.7%
Economy: Services 57.8%, Industry 29.4%, Agriculture 12.8%

How important is American consumerism to the country?

The United States is the most important export market for the emerging Sri Lankan economy. After 26 years of war, the country has begun to build itself up to higher living standards in the last three years, through means such as private enterprise and manufacturing. For these purposes, the U.S market is a crucial source of income in the country.

Products from Sri Lanka (*Company of local origin)

Apparel: *Adidas, Liz Claiborne, Nike, Reebok, Triumph International*
BAT: *British American Tobacco*
Some coffee, tea and spices are also imported from Sri Lanka.

Did you know?

Sri Lanka used to be called Ceylon.

Human rights

A quarter-century long civil war finally came to an end in 2009, leaving government to reform itself and begin investigations into possible war crimes and human rights violations. Some reports of attacks on civil society, arbitrary detention and torture were still reported in 2010, according to Human Rights Watch. Trafficking in persons, limits on workers' rights, and child labor remain problems, according to the State Department. The government fails to adequately protect the right to strike, and union activists and officials are subject to harassment, intimidation, and other retaliatory practices. Labor organizations report that employers in export processing zones frequently failed to pay workers their wages due when downsizing or closing factories.

Environment

In the EPI, Sri Lanka's scores come in above the averages for both its region and its income group. Problems are mostly caused by air pollution and disease, but it is assessed positively for its environmental performance.

Tourism

There are no available records of how many U.S. tourists visit Sri Lanka.

SWEDEN

TRADE RATIO: 0.49

U.S. TRADE BALANCE WITH SWEDEN	SWEDEN'S MAIN TRADE PARTNERS
Deficit of $5.8 billion	*Exports:* Norway 10.6%, Germany
Exports to Sweden: $4.7 billion	10.2%, United Kingdom 7.4%
Imports to U.S.: $10.5 billion	*Imports:* Germany 18%,
Government Type: Constitutional	Denmark 8.9%, Norway 8.7%
monarchy	*Economy:* Services 71.6%,
Population: 9 million	Industry 26.6%,
Unemployment: 8.4%	Agriculture 1.9%

How important is American consumerism to the country?
United States is the sixth biggest export destination for Swedish goods, with a 6% share, including many consumer products, such as electronics, furniture and vehicles, but much of Swedish imports are things for industrial use, such as machinery and medical equipment.

Products from Sweden (*Company of local origin)
Volvo*, Saab*, IKEA*, Ericsson*, Electrolux*, H&M*, Scania*, Husqvarna*

Did you know?
Sweden is the world's third largest exporter of pop music, after the U.S. and the United Kingdom.
Swedes are very inventive and claim, among many inventions made in the country, the zipper, the refrigerator, the computer mouse, and the pacemaker.

Human rights
Sweden is ranked 4th in Transparency International's Corruption Index, indicating nearly no corruption at all. They share first place in the World Press Freedom Index, and are categorized as a model free democracy.

Environment
Sweden comes in 4th in the world in EPI's country comparison, with an excellent overall environmental record.

Tourism
Sweden was visited by 228,000 Americans in 2009.

SWITZERLAND

TRADE RATIO: 1.08

U.S. TRADE BALANCE WITH SWITZERLAND
Surplus of $1.55 billion
Exports to Switzerland: $20.7 billion
Imports to U.S.: $19.1 billion
Government Type: Republic
Population: 7.6 million
Unemployment: 3.9%

SWITZERLAND'S MAIN TRADE PARTNERS
Exports: Germany 19.3%, USA 10.1%, Italy 8.4%
Imports: Germany 32.6%, Italy 10.7%, France 9.3%
Economy: Services 71.1%, Industry 27.7%, Agriculture 1.3%

How important is American consumerism to the country?
U.S. is the second largest export destination for Swiss goods, with a 10% share—behind neighboring Germany. Switzerland mostly exports high-quality consumer goods, high technology machinery and pharmaceuticals. Their service industry, especially the banking industry, plays a large role in their economy.

Products from Switzerland (*Company of local origin)
Nestlé*, Logitech*, TAG Heuer*, Swatch*, Movenpick*, Rolex, Novartis* (pharmaceuticals)

Did you know?
Switzerland is a world leader in chemical and pharmaceutical production. Their chemical industry has its focus mainly in production of dye-stuffs, food flavorings and perfume essences. 85% of these industries' output is exported. [37]
In terms of value, Switzerland is responsible for about half of the world's watch production.
Nestlé, one of the world's largest food companies, is headquartered in Switzerland.

Environment
Switzerland comes second to only Iceland in EPI's comparison of environmental performance. Their commitment to preserving their own country's environment, as well as their pollution and emissions standards, is extremely high.

Tourism
Nearly 500,000 Americans visited Switzerland in 2009, the last year that statistics are currently available for travel there. This makes it the 23rd most popular travel destination for American residents.

TAIWAN

TRADE RATIO: 0.73

U.S. TRADE BALANCE WITH TAIWAN

Deficit of $9.8 billion
Exports to Taiwan: $26 billion
Imports to U.S.: $35.9 billion

Government Type: Republic
Population: 23 million
Unemployment: 5.2%

TAIWAN'S MAIN TRADE PARTNERS

Exports: China 28.1%, Hong Kong 13.8%, USA 11.5%
Imports: Japan 20.7%, China 14.2%, USA 10%
Economy: Services 67.5%, Industry 31.1%, Agriculture 1.4%

How important is American consumerism to the country?
The United States receives over 11% of all Taiwanese exports, making it the third largest export market for Taiwan. Exports include electronics, high technology goods, machinery for industrial use, sub-assemblies for electronics and textiles and apparel.

Products from Taiwan (*Company of local origin)
Acer*, Asus*, D-Link*
Foreign companies with manufacturing facilities in Taiwan: *Mazda, Yamaha, 3Com, Logitech, Siemens, Bridgestone/Firestone, Levi Strauss, Nike, Gucci, Reebok, Procter & Gamble*

Did you know?
Taiwan is one of the world's largest producers of computer technology.
Taiwan is an island just off the coast of mainland China. They have been effectively independent since 1949 but China refuses to acknowledge this. Therefore China has prevented any other country from having official diplomatic ties with Taiwan.
Taiwan is a major buyer of arms, mostly supplied by the United States.

Human rights
Taiwan comes in at 33rd in Transparency International's corruption index, comparing very favorably with "uncle" China, which ranks 78th on the list.
Freedom House ranks Taiwan as an exceptionally free country, determining that its citizens enjoy the highest grade of civil and political liberties.

Environment
Taiwan is not ranked in Yale's EPI index at all, but it placed bottom of the heap in 130th place in its precursor list, the Environmental Sustainability Index (ESI) in 2005. Improvements have been made but it is difficult to compare to the other countries on the list as it was not included in the 2010 comparison.

Tourism
576,000 Americans visited Taiwan in 2009 according to the Office of Travel and Tourism Industries.

THAILAND

TRADE RATIO: 0.39

U.S TRADE BALANCE WITH THAILAND
Deficit of $13.7 billion in 2010
Exports to Thailand: $8.9 billion
Imports to U.S.: $22.7 billion
Government: Constitutional monarchy, ruled by King Bhumibol since 1946.
Population: 67 million
Unemployment: 1.1%

THAILAND'S MAIN TRADE PARTNERS
Exports: USA 10.9%, China 10.6%, Japan 10.3
Imports: Japan 18.7%, China 12.7%, Malaysia 6.4%
Economy: Industry 44.7%, Services 42.9%, Agriculture 12.4%

How important is American consumerism to the country?
The United States is Thailand's largest export destination. More than 10% of their exports end up in America, chiefly apparel, fish and seafood, rice and rubber products, and electronics.

Products from Thailand (*Company of local origin):
Electronics, fish & seafood, especially shrimp (Thailand is America's top source of shrimp), footwear, textiles, apparel

Did you know?
Thailand is the world's leading exporter of canned tuna, with 31% of the world's canned tuna exports (the U.S. is the largest export destination for this tuna).[38]
Thailand is also the world's top exporter of rubber.[39]

Human rights
Thailand has a relatively authoritarian government. Freedom House reports that the government used violent means to put down protests in 2010 and has also limited freedom of expression and personal autonomy in the country. Transparency International also reports corruption problems in the country.

Environment
Thailand ranks near the middle of the pack in the EPI study. Air pollution, the state of its fisheries (mainly due to trawling), as well as high carbon emissions lower their score.

Tourism
Tourism is a crucially important part of the economy, with more than 15 million visitors each year. Many Americans visit as well—In 2009 some 364,000 Americans visited, making it the 28th most popular destination for U.S. residents.

TRINIDAD & TOBAGO

TRADE RATIO: 0.29

U.S. TRADE BALANCE WITH TRINIDAD

Deficit of $4.7 billion
Exports to Trinidad & Tobago:
$1.9 billion
Imports to U.S.: $6.6 billion

Government Type: Republic
Population: 1.2 million
Unemployment: 6.4%

TRINIDAD & TOBAGO MAIN TRADE PARTNERS

Exports: USA 42.2%, Spain 7.6%, Jamaica 4.8%
Imports: USA 32.6%, Russia 10%, Colombia 6.2%
Economy: Industry 58.8%, Services 40.8%, Agriculture 0.4%

How important is American consumerism to the country?
The U.S. is the largest export market for goods from Trinidad & Tobago. However, 80% of exports to America are petroleum products. Most of the other exports are also raw materials.

Products from Trinidad & Tobago (*Company of local origin)
Beverages, cereal products, sugar, cocoa, coffee, citrus, vegetables, flowers

Did you know?
Trinidad & Tobago is one of the wealthiest countries in the Caribbean. Natural gas is the main export.

Human rights
Trinidad is a free country with a fast-developing economy, uplifting its citizens' living standards. Press freedom is commendable and citizens enjoy a wide range of political and civil rights.

Environment
Trinidad & Tobago, a fast growing Caribbean nation, ranks 103rd out of 163 countries in the EPI comparison. It is given a score well below the average for other nations in its income group, as well as a below average score for the Americas.

Tourism
Over 100,000 U.S. citizens visit the country annually, making up about 30% of the number of tourists visiting Trinidad & Tobago.

TURKEY

TRADE RATIO: 2.50

U.S. TRADE BALANCE WITH TURKEY	TURKEY'S MAIN TRADE PARTNERS
Surplus of $6.3 billion	*Exports:* Germany 9.6%, France 6.1%, United Kingdom 5.8%
Exports to Turkey: $10.5 billion	
Imports to U.S.: $4.2 billion	*Imports:* Russia 13.8%, Germany 10%, China 9%
Government Type: Republic	*Economy:* Services 63.8%, Industry 26.6%, Agriculture 9.6%
Population: 79 million	
Unemployment: 12%	

How important is American consumerism to the country?
The United States is not among Turkey's major export destinations, as most of their exports head to Europe. Textiles and apparel form the major part of the consumer goods Turkey brings to America, as well as vehicles.

Products from Turkey (*Company of local origin)
Vehicles: *Toyota, Daimler, Ford, GM, Honda*
Tobacco: *Philip Morris* (Marlboro, Virginia Slims, B&H, etc.), *BAT* (Lucky Strike, Kent, Pall Mall), *Imperial Tobacco Group* (West, Gitanes, Gauloises, Fortuna etc.)
Apparel: *Adidas, Benetton, Dolce & Gabbana, Levi's, Nike, Reebok*, etc.

Did you know?
There are more than 5 million Turks working and living in other European countries. Turkey is an important NATO ally for the United States.

Human rights
Press freedom is sometimes lacking in Turkey, where journalists have been imprisoned or brought to court, most of them of either the minority Kurd ethnicity or covering Kurd issues. Freedom House ranks Turkey as "partly free"—democratic elections exist and there is not a great deal of corruption.

Environment
Turkey is ranked 77th in the world in the 2010 EPI comparison. Protection of biodiversity and critical habitats, the state of their fisheries and high greenhouse emissions are the main issues cited by the researchers.

Tourism
Close to 400,000 visitors from America travel to Turkey each year. Tourism is a strong source of income for Turkey.

UNITED ARAB EMIRATES

TRADE RATIO: 10.2

U.S. TRADE BALANCE WITH UAE	UAE'S MAIN TRADE PARTNERS
Surplus of $10.5 billion	*Exports:* Japan 17.5%, India 11.9%, South Korea 7.2%
Exports to UAE: $11.7 billion	*Imports:* India 15%, China 13.5%, USA 8.8%
Imports to U.S.: $1.1 billion	
Government Type: Federation of monarchies	*Economy:* Industry 53%, Services 46.1%, Agriculture 0.9%
Population: 5 million	
Unemployment: 2.4%	

How important is American consumerism to the country?

UAE exports little to the United States and next to no consumer goods at all. Exports mostly consist of precious stones, minerals and oil. They do, however, import much more from the United States, supporting our industries' machinery, bulldozers, jet engines, air conditioning equipment, airplanes and vehicles.

Products from United Arab Emirates (*Company of local origin)

Oil

Did you know?

United Arab Emirates is a federation of seven monarchies, governed by the Emir of Abu Dhabi, the richest Sheikhdom of the seven that compose UAE.

Human rights

UAE is not a democracy, and not a free country. People do not vote for their leaders. However, because of the high degree of wealth and non-existent unemployment in the area, there are few signs of uprising or dissatisfaction. Corruption is low, UAE being ranked just below the United Kingdom in that regard. Freedom of speech and freedom of the press are limited.

Environment

UAE ranks near the bottom in the EPI comparison. Especially problematic are water supply questions, lack of marine protection and overfishing, as well as high carbon emissions. However, many of the sheikdoms are investing in renewable energies to prepare for a future after their oil runs out.

Tourism

257,000 Americans traveled to UAE in 2009.

UNITED KINGDOM

TRADE RATIO: 0.97

U.S. TRADE BALANCE WITH U.K.	U.K.'S MAIN TRADE PARTNERS
Deficit of $1.4 billion	*Exports:* USA 14.7%, Germany 11.1%, France 8%
Exports to U.K.: $48.4 billion	*Imports:* Germany 12.9%, USA 9.7%, China 8.9%
Imports to U.S.: $49.8 billion	
Government Type: Constitutional monarchy	*Economy:* Services 77.5%, Industry 21.8%, Agriculture 0.7%
Population: 63 million	
Unemployment: 7.8%	

How important is American consumerism to the country?

The U.S. is the number 1 export destination of the United Kingdom, with a 14% share. The close relationship with the two countries and active trade relations mean the U.S. is the key market for the United Kingdom.

Products from United Kingdom (*Company of local origin)

British American Tobacco (BAT)*, Aston Martin*, Rover*, Rolls Royce*, Bentley*, Cadbury*, Virgin Group*, Dyson Applicances*, Travelodge*, BBC*, Sky*, The Economist*, Oxfam* (non-profit), O2*, Imperial Tobacco*

Did you know?

The United Kingdom is the sixth largest manufacturer in the world.
The British drink more tea than any other nation on the planet—over twenty times more than Americans do.
The first inhabitants to the island arrived about 10,000 years ago.
It is the third most populous island in the world, with a population of about 60 million.

Environment

The U.K. is judged to be doing well in its environmental policy. It ranks 14th in the 2010 Environmental Performance Index, indicating it is on track to meet internationally recognized environmental policy goals.

Tourism

In 2010 about 2.4 million Americans visited Britain, the 3rd most popular tourist destination after Mexico and Canada.

VENEZUELA

TRADE RATIO: 0.32

U.S. TRADE BALANCE WITH VENEZUELA	VENEZUELA'S MAIN TRADE PARTNERS
Deficit of $22 billion	*Exports:* USA 37.8%, China 5.8%, Singapore 4.9%
Exports to Venezuela: $10.6 billion	*Imports:* USA 27.1%, Colombia 11.8%, China 8.6%
Imports to U.S.: $32.7 billion	*Economy:* Services 60%, Industry 36%, Agriculture 4%
Government Type: Republic	
Population: 27 million	
Unemployment: 8.5%	

How important is American consumerism to the country?
The United States is by far the largest export destination of Venezuela, accounting for nearly a third of all exports. This includes minerals and especially petroleum, which makes up a whopping 95% of all export revenues.

Products from Venezuela (*Company of local origin)
Oil, minerals

Did you know?
Venezuela now reportedly has the world's largest oil reserves, and it is the 8th largest producer of oil in the world.[40] In spite of that, some economists are concerned that the country may well go bankrupt in the next several years thanks to dubious financial policies by their authoritarian president, Hugo Chavez.[41]

Human rights
President Hugo Chavez has been in power since 1999 and recently passed a vote eliminating all term limits for the presidency, effectively keeping himself in power indefinitely. Freedom in Venezuela has been tumbling during Chavez's presidency, and their scores in Freedom of the World 2011 were lower than in previous evaluations. Freedom of the Press is especially suppressed in Venezuela today.
Venezuela also ranks near the bottom in the Corruption Index, coming in 164th out of 178 countries. Only the most corrupt and failed states, like Sudan and Afghanistan, came in with worse scores.

Environment
In their environmental policies, Venezuela is near the middle of the pack. They are nearly tied with Brazil and the United States, and rank 64th in the world in the EPI comparison.

Tourism
143,000 Americans traveled to Venezuela in 2009.

VIETNAM

TRADE RATIO: 0.25

U.S. TRADE BALANCE WITH VIETNAM
Deficit of $11 billion
Exports to Vietnam: $3.7 billion
Imports to U.S.: $14.9 billion
Government Type: *Communist republic*
Population: 90 million
Unemployment: 4.4%

VIETNAM'S MAIN TRADE PARTNERS
Exports: USA 20%, Japan 10.7%, China 9.8%
Imports: China 23.8%, South Korea 11.6%, Japan 10.8%
Economy: Industry 41.1%, Services 38.3%, Agriculture 20.6%

How important is American consumerism to the country?
The U.S. is the largest export partner for Vietnam, accounting for just over one-fifth of all their exports. Most of these exports are consumer goods like clothing, shoes and consumer electronics assembled there.

Products from Vietnam (*Company of local origin)
Nearly all major apparel brands, *British American Tobacco, IKEA, Gillette, Colgate, Daewoo, Unilever*

Did you know?
Vietnam is the largest producer of *Nike* shoes, making 37% of all the company's footwear—China comes second and Indonesia third—in fact, these three countries manufacture 94% of all *Nike* shoes.[42]

Human rights
Civil and political freedoms are somewhat weak in Vietnam. Poverty has declined greatly since the 1980s with economic focus on manufacturing being added and a more capitalist approach having been applied in the country, although income inequality has predictably increased as a result.
Press freedom is also weak, Vietnam ranking in the bottom 15 in Reporters Without Borders' study from last year. Corruption is also a problem.

Environment
Vietnam ranks near the bottom of the EPI comparison as well. The state of their fisheries is a concern, with excessive trawling for their seafood exports a cause, along with air pollution and loss of habitat and biodiversity.

Tourism
182,000 Americans visited Vietnam in 2009, ranking it 37th for Americans' destinations.

NOTES

Introduction

1 Bradley Blackburn and Eric Noll, "Made in America: A Brief History of U.S. Manufacturing," ABC News, Feb. 2011, http://abcnews.go.com/Business/made-america-middle-class-built-manufacturing-jobs/story?id=12916118.

2 Annie Baxter, "Consumer Spending Accounts for Two-Thirds of U.S. Economy," *Minnesota Public Radio*, October 2008, http://minnesota.publicradio.org/display/web/2008/10/29/gdp_numbers_consumer_spending/.

Chapter 1: The Way Forward

1 *CIA World Factbook*, 2011, https://www.cia.gov/library/publications/the-world-factbook/rankorder/2087rank.html?countryName=United%20States&countryCode=us&regionCode=noa&rank=1#us.

2 Amanda Terkel, "With Recession Looming, Bush Tells America to "Go Shopping More," *Think Progress*, Dec. 2006, http://thinkprogress.org/politics/2006/12/20/9281/bush-shopping/.

Chapter 2: A Business Owner's Perspective

1 "How Important Are Small Businesses to the U.S. Economy?", *U.S. Small Business Administration*, http://www.sba.gov/advocacy/7495/8420.

2 James Cooper, "3 Million High Paying Jobs (or more) Lost Forever, *The Fiscal Times*, May 2011, http://www.thefiscaltimes.com/Columns/2011/05/16/3-Million-High-Paying-Jobs-or%20more-Lost-Forever.aspx#page1.

3 David Wessel, "Big U.S. Firms Shift Hiring Abroad," *The Wall Street Journal*, April 19, 2011.

Chapter 3: The Importance of U.S. Manufacturing

1 Bill Moyers, "Welcome to the Plutocracy!", speech at Boston University on October 29, 2010, accessed online at http://archive.truthout.org/bill-moyers-money-fights-hard-and-it-fights-dirty64766.

2 Ronald. R. Pollina, *Selling Out a Superpower: Where the U.S. Economy Went Wrong and How We Can Turn It Around* (New York: Prometheus Books, 2010), p.46.

3 Michael Ettlinger and Kate Gordon, "The Importance and Promise of American Manufacturing," *Center for American Progress*, April 2011, p.5.

4 Michael Ettlinger and Kate Gordon, "The Importance and Promise of American Manufacturing," *Center for American Progress*, April 2011, p. 9.

5 Robert E. Scott, "Growing U.S. Trade Deficit with China Cost 2.8 million jobs between 2001 and 2010," *Economic Policy Institute*, September 2011, http://www.epi.org/publication/growing-trade-deficit-china-cost-2-8-million/.

6 Robert E. Scott, "Costly Trade with China," *Economic Policy Institute*, October 2007, http://www.epi.org/publication/bp188/.

7 Ian Fletcher, *Free Trade Doesn't Work: What Should Replace It and Why* (Washington: U.S. Business and Industry Council, 2010), p. 57.

8 Elizabeth McNichol et al., "States Continue to Fell Recession's Impact," *Center on Budget and Policy Priorities*, June 17, 2011, http://www.cbpp.org/cms/?fa=view&id=711.

9 Deficit numbers from *U.S. Census Bureau, Foreign Trade Statistics.*

10 Congressman Sherrod Brown, *Myths of Free Trade: Why American Trade Policy Has Failed* (New York: The New Press, 2006), p.151.

11 Justin Lahart, "Tallying the Toll of U.S.-China Trade," *Wall Street Journal*, September 27, 2011.

12 Clyde Prestowitz, *The Betrayal of American Prosperity: Free Market Delusions, America's Decline, and How We Must Compete in the Post-Dollar Era* (New York: Free Press, 2010), p. 2.

13 Bureau of Labor Statistics, http://www.bls.gov/webapps/legacy/cesbtab1.htm.

14 Richard A, McCormack, "U.S. Is Virtually A Non-Player in the Solar Power Production Business," Manufacturing & Technology News, January 10, 2008, vol. 15, no. 1, http://www.manufacturingnews.com/news/08/0110/art1.html.

15 "Industrial Metamorphosis," *The Economist,* September 29, 2005.

16 Michael Mandel, "The Real Cost of Offshoring," *BusinessWeek*, June 18, 2007.

17 Joseph Kahn, "Ruse in Toyland : Chinese Workers' Hidden Woe," *The New York Times*, December 7, 2003.

18 Senator Byron Dorgan, *Take This Job and Ship It! How Corporate Greed and Brain Dead Politics Are Selling Out America* (New York: Thomas Dunne Books, 2006. pp. 139-142.

19 "Industrial Metamorphosis," The Economist, September 29, 2005.

20 Clyde Prestowitz, The Betrayal of American Prosperity: Free Market Delusions, America's Decline, and How We Must Compete in the Post-Dollar Era (New York: Free Press, 2010). p.26.

21 Ian Fletcher, Free Trade Doesn't Work: What Should Replace It and Why (Washington: U.S. Business and Industry Council, 2010), p. 67.

22 Richard J. Elkus Jr., *Winner Take All: How Competitiveness Shapes the Fate of Nations* (Basic Books, 2008), pp.75-76.

23 Clyde Prestowitz, The Betrayal of American Prosperity: Free Market Delusions, America's Decline, and How We Must Compete in the Post-Dollar Era (New York: Free Press, 2010), p.253.

24 Richard A. McCormack, "The Plight of American Manufacturing," in Manufacturing a Better Future for America, Richard McCormack, ed. (Washington: The Alliance for American Manufacturing, 2009), p.6.

25 Erica Fuchs, "Design for Location? The Impact of Manufacturing Offshore on Technology Competitiveness in the Optoelectronics Industry," *Management Science*, Vol. 56, no. 12, pp 2323-2349.

26 Gary P. Pisano and Willy C. Shih, "The U.S. Must Manufacture In Order to Innovate," *Harvard Business Review*, November 17, 2009, http://blogs.hbr.org/hbr/restoring-american-competitiveness/2009/11/the-us-must-manufacture.html.

27 Michael Mandel, "The GDP Mirage," *BusinessWeek,* October 29, 2009.

28 James Dyson, "China: The Intellectual Property Battleground," *Bloomberg Businessweek*, February 16, 2011.

29 U.S. Census Bureau, Foreign Trade Statistics, http://www.census.gov/foreign-trade/balance/.

30 Steve Lohr, "G.E. Goes with What It Knows: Making Stuff, *The New York Times*, December 4, 2010.

31 Bureau of Labor Statistics, http://www.bls.gov/webapps/legacy/cesbtab1.htm.

32 USA State and Country QuickFacts, *United States Census Bureau.*

33 Ian Fletcher, "America's Trade Deficit Is, Too, Real Money," *Huffington Post*, February 15, 2011.

34 Warren E. Buffett, "America's Growing Trade Deficit Is Selling the Nation Out From Under Us." *Fortune*, November 10, 2003.

35 Chris Isidore, "Economists Biggest Worry: Federal Budget Deficit," CNN Money, February 28, 2011.

Chapter 4: How Competing Countries Are Succeeding

1 Christian Reiermann, "Industry Returns As Economic Engine," *Spiegel Online International,* December 2, 2008.

2 Scott Paul, "We're Number Two: Why America Is Losing Its Lead in Manufacturing," *The Huffington Post*, March 16, 2011.

3 Harold Meyerson, "Business Is Booming," *The American Prospect*, January 28, 2011.

4 Christian Vits, "Germany to Regain World's Second-Biggest Exporter Spot, Ifo Says," *Bloomberg*, April 19, 2011.

5 Jana Randow, "German Exports Surge to Record $141.4 billion in March, Boosting Growth," *Bloomberg,* May 8, 2011.

6 Rainer Buergin and Christian Vits, "German Unemployment Falls Below 3 Million to 19-Year Low," *Bloomberg Businessweek*, April 28, 2011.

7 Henk Bekker, "List of 20 Best-Selling Car Manufacturers in Germany in 2010," *Suite101*, http://henk-bekker.suite101.com/list-of-20-best-selling-car-manufacturers -in-germany-in-2010-a328223.

8 Ford Automotive Operations Europe (Germany), *Ford.com,* http://media.ford.com/ article_display.cfm?article_id=29.

9 Jeremy Korzeniewski, "America's Best Selling Cars And Trucks of 2010 Are...," *Autoblog,* http://www.autoblog.com/2011/01/04/americas-best-selling-cars-and-trucks-of-2010-are/.

10 "Consumer Appliances in Germany", *Euromonitor International*, Country Report, May 2011.

11 Louis Uchitelle, "When Factories Vanish, So Can Innovation," *The New York Times*, February 12, 2011.

12 "Outsourcing Made in Germany," *Deutsche Welle*, July 22, 2004.

13 Andreas Knorr and Andreas Arndt, "Why Did Wal-Mart Fail in Germany?", *University of Bremen*, 2003.

14 Mark Landler, "Wal-Mart Decides to Pull Out of Germany," *The New York Times*, July 28, 2006.

15 Bruce Nussbaum, "Is the Wal-Mart Model Dead?", *BusinessWeek,* November 30, 2006.

16 Christian Reiermann, "Industry Returns As Economic Engine," *Spiegel Online Inte rnational,* December 2, 2008.

17 Ibid

18 Harold Meyerson, "Business Is Booming," *The American Prospect*, January 28, 2011.

19 Christian Reiermann, "Industry Returns As Economic Engine," *Spiegel Online International,* December 2, 2008.

20 "China, Germany Sign Deals Worth Billions of Dollars, Say Trade Strong Despite Financial Crisis," *China Daily*, July 16, 2010.

21 Eamonn Fingleton, "Germany's Economic Engine," *The American Prospect*, February 24, 2010.

22 Ian Fletcher, "What the U.S Can Learn From Germany About Managing Its Trade Deficit," *Seeking Alpha*, June 2010, http://seekingalpha.com/article/ 212461-what-the-u-s-can-learn-from-germany-about-managing-its-trade-deficit.

23 Derek Thompson, "Is Japan's Debt Doomed?", *The Atlantic*, March 14, 2011.

24 "Major Foreign Holders of Treasury Securities," *United States Department of the Treasury Resource Center*, September 2011, http://www.treasury.gov/resource-center/ data-chart-center/tic/Documents/mfh.txt.

25 "Japan's Manufacturing Competitiveness Strategy: Challenges for Japan, Opportunities for the United States," *United States Department of Commerce International Trade Commission* April 1, 2009.

26 Ian Fletcher, "What the U.S. Can Learn From Germany About Managing Its Trade Deficit," *Seeking Alpha*, June 2010, http://seekingalpha.com/article/212461-what-the-u-s-can-learn-from-germany-about-managing-its-trade-deficit.

27 Clyde Prestowitz, *The Betrayal of American Prosperity: Free Market Delusions, America's Decline, and How We Must Compete in the Post-Dollar Era* (New York: Free Press, 2010), p.97.

28 Zeynep Gürhan-Canli and Durairaj Maheswaran, "Cultural Variations in Country of Origin Effects," *Journal of Marketing Research*, August 2000, 37, 3.

29 Wayne D. Hoyer and Deborah J. McInnis, *Consumer Behavior*, p. 115, (South Western College Pub., 2006).

30 "Japan Isn't Buying the Wal-Mart Idea," *BusinessWeek*, February 28, 2005.

31 Mariko Sanchanta, "Wal-Mart Japan CEO Resigns," *The Wall Street Journal*, June 20, 2011.

32 William J. Holstein, "Why Wal-Mart Can't Find Happiness in Japan," *Fortune*, July 27, 2007.

33 John J. Watson and Katrina Wright, "Consumer Ethnocentrism and Attitudes Towards Domestic and Foreign Products", *European Journal of Marketing*, vol. 34, no. 9/10, 2000, pp.1149–1166.

34 Maznah Ghazali et al., "Products and Country of Origin Effects: The Malaysian Consumers' Perception," *International Review of Business Research Papers*, Vol 4. No. 2 March 2008, pp. 91-102.

35 "Trade in Goods with Japan," *U.S Census Bureau Foreign Trade Statistics*, http://www.census.gov/foreign-trade/balance/c5880.html .

36 Clyde Prestowitz, "Why Isn't the iPhone Made in America?", *Foreign Policy*, March 8, 2011, http://prestowitz.foreignpolicy.com/posts/2011/03/08/why_isnt_the_iphone_made_in_america.

37 Ha-Joon Chang, *23 Things They Don't Tell You About Capitalism* (New York: Bloomsbury Press, 2010), p.152.

38 Ha-Joon Chang, *Bad Samaritans: The Myth of Free Trade and the Secret History of Capitalism* (New York: Bloomsbury Press, 2008), p.3.

39 Ibid.

40 Laura C. Nelson, *Measured Excess: Status, Gender and Consumer Nationalism in South Korea* (Columbia University Press, 2000).

41 CIA World Factbook, 2011, https://www.cia.gov/library/publications/the-world-factbook/rankorder/2078rank.html?countryName=Korea,%20South&countryCode=ks&regionCode=eas&rank=8#ks.

42 Per Capita GDP in U.S. Dollars," United Nations Statistics Division, National Accounts Main Aggregates Database, http://unstats.un.org/unsd/snaama/dnllist.asp.

43 CIA World Factbook, 2011,accessed at https://www.cia.gov/library/publications/the-world-factbook/geos/ks.html.

44 Linsu Kim, *Imitation to Innovation: The Dynamics of Korea's Technological Learning*, (Boston: Harvard Business School Press, 1997), p.2.

45 Ha-Joon Chang, *Bad Samaritans: The Myth of Free Trade and the Secret History of Capitalism* (New York: Bloomsbury Press, 2008), pp.6-9.

46 "South Korea's Export Competitiveness: Critical to Overcoming the Global Crisis and Issues Going Forward," *Bank of Tokyo-Mitsubishi UFJ Economic Review*, Vol. 5, No. 2, February 2010.

47 "Exports of Goods and Services (% of GDP)," *The World Bank Databank*, http://data.worldbank.org/indicator/NE.EXP.GNFS.ZS.

48 Mark Osborne, "Semiconductor Industry Set for Explosive Growth, says Future Horizons," *Fabtech*, November 3, 2009, http://www.fabtech.org/news/_a/semiconductor_industry_set_for_explosive_growth_says_future_horizons/.

49 Ümit Engínsoy, "Korean Miracle Result of Export-Oriented Industry, Discipline," *Hurriyet Daily News*, June 30, 2010.

50 "South Korea – Shipbuilding": *Library of Congress Country Study Series*, http://www.country-data.com/cgi-bin/query/r-12311.html.

51 Lee Jong-Heon, "South Korean Shipyards Anticipate Orders," *UPI Asia.com*, April 21, 2009, http://www.upiasia.com/Economics/2009/04/21/south_korean_shipyards_anticipate_orders/2568/.

52 "2010 Production Statistics," *International Organization of Motor Vehicle Manufacturers*, http://oica.net/category/production-statistics/.

53 Kim Soo-yeon, "Rate Hike Heralds Start of Korea's Stimulus Exit," *YonHap News*, July 9, 2010.

54 Ha-Joon Chang, *Bad Samaritans: The Myth of Free Trade and the Secret History of Capitalism* (New York: Bloomsbury Press, 2008), pp.2-3, 210.

55 Ha-Joon Chang, *Bad Samaritans : The Myth of Free Trade and the Secret History of Capitalism* (New York: Bloomsbury Press, 2008), p.7.

56 Ibid.

57 Ibid.

58 Laura C. Nelson, *Measured Excess: Status, Gender and Consumer Nationalism in South Korea* (Columbia University Press, 2000), pp. 2-3.

Chapter 5: The Label Game

1 "Complying with the Made in USA Standard," *Bureau of Consumer Protection BusinessCenter*,http://business.ftc.gov/documents/bus03-complying-made-usa-standard.

2 "How iPhones Are Produced," ADB Institute, http://www.adbi.org/working-paper/2010/12/14/4236.iphone.widens.us.trade.deficit.prc/how.iphones.are.produced/.

3 "FTC Proposed Guides for the Use of U.S. Origin Claims," *Federal Trade Commission*, http://www.ftc.gov/opa/1997/05/examples.shtm.

4 "Made-in-USA Toys Hard to Find," *CBS News*, February 11, 2009, http://www.cbsnews.com/stories/2003/12/23/world/main589970.shtml.

5 Sarah Lorge Butler, "An American Girl Doll Moves Down the Hall," *CBS Money Watch*, July 7, 2010, http://moneywatch.bnet.com/saving-money/blog/family-finance/an-american-girl-doll-moves-in-down-the-hall/2560/.

6 "Consumer Reports Investigates the Truth Behind Labels That Imply "Made in the USA,"*Consumer Reports*, February 4, 2008.

7 "Is It Really Made in the USA: Behind the Label Claims," *Daily Finance*, http://www.dailyfinance.com/photos/made-in-the-usa-truth-behind-the-labels/3659457/.

8 Byron L. Dorgan, *Take This Job and Ship It: How Corporate Greed and Brain-Dead Politics Are Selling Out America* (New York: Thomas Dunne Books, 2006), pp.31-32.

9 www.pennsylvaniahouse.com.

10 Daniel Robison, "Made in America Store Capitalizes on Patriotism," *NPR*, June 22, 2011

11 "That Luxury Item May Be Made in China, *American Public Media Marketplace*, February 2, 2009, http://www.marketplace.org/topics/business/luxury-item-may-be-made-china.

12 Ibid.

13 Dana Thomas, "Made in China on the Sly," *The New York Times*, November 23, 2007.

14 Ibid.

15 Sara Bongiorni, *A Year Without Made in China: One Family's True Life Adventure in the Global Economy* (Wiley, 2009), p.54.

16 "U.S. E-Retail Sales 2009-2015," *Internet Retailer*, http://www.internetretailer.com/trends/sales/.

17 Mark Tran, "Nike Toes the Line," *The Guardian*, April 13, 2005.

18 "Active Factories", *Nike*, http://www.nikebiz.com/responsibility/documents/factory_disclosure_list.pdf.

19 "Levi Strauss & Co. Factory List," http://www.levistrauss.com/sites/default/files/librarydocument/2011/9/lsco-factory-list-may-2011a.pdf.

20 Byron L. Dorgan, *Take This Job and Ship It: How Corporate Greed and Brain-Dead Politics Are Selling Out America* (New York: Thomas Dunne Books, 2006), p.56.

21 http://www.shopnewbalance.com/information/madeinusa.asp?s1=NBAS&s2=madeinusa.

Chapter 6: Information You Need When You Need It

1 "Mandatory Country of Origin Labeling–Final Rule," *USDA*, http://www.ams.usda.gov/AMSv1.0/getfile?dDocName=STELPRDC5074847.

2 "Resolution on Country of Origin Labeling," Trans Atlantic Consumer Dialogue, Doc No. Food 29-08, March 2008, http://tacd.org/index2.php?option=com_docman&task=doc_view&gid=39&Itemid=.

3 "FDA Aims to Boost Import Safety," *USA Today*, June 21, 2011.

4 Ibid.

5 Brad Racino, "Flood of Food Imported to U.S., But Only 2 Percent Inspected," *MSNBC.com*, October 3, 2011, http://www.msnbc.msn.com/id/44701433/ns/health-food_safety/t/flood-food-imported-us-only-percent-inspected/#.TqnQ8ptCqso.

6 Joshua P. Berning et al., "Identifying Consumer Preferences for Nutrition Information on Grocery Store Shelf Labels," *Food Marketing Policy Center*, Research Report no. 120, December 2009.

7 Ioana G. Carabin and Bernardene A. Magnuson, "New Labeling Requirements for Food Allergens," *Nutritional Outlook*, April 4, 2006.

8 Brad Stone and Bruce Einhorn, "How Baidu Won China," *Bloomberg Businessweek*, November 11, 2010.

9 Juanita S. Kavalauskas and Charles J. Kahane, Ph.D., "Evaluation of the American Automobile Labeling Act," *National Highway Traffic Safety Administration*, 2001, http://www.nhtsa.gov/cars/rules/regrev/evaluate/809208.html.

10 Ibid.

11 Bryan Chee, "The Grille Says USA, But That Car Is an Import. Or Is It?," *autobytel.com*, June 28th, 2006, http://www.autobytel.com/car-buying-guides/features/made-in-america-1969/.

12 http://www.toyota.com/about/our_business/our_numbers images/2010USOperations Brochure.pdf.

13 http://www.bmwusfactory.com/.

14 http://mbusi.com/.

15 Madeleine Bunting, "Sweatshops Are Still Supplying High Street Brands," *The Guardian*, April 28, 2011.

Chapter 7: The Transparent Label

1 Malcolm Moore, "Inside Foxconn's Suicide Factory", *The Telegraph*, May 27, 2010.

2 Ralph Jennings, "Foxconn Plans Brazil Factory for Apple Products," *PC World, April 14, 2011*, http://www.pcworld.com/article/225185/foxconn_plans_brazil_factory_for_apple_products.html.

3 Ninelu Tu and Joseph Tsai, "Foxconn denies passing up Nook orders in exchange for Microsoft lawsuit withdrawal", *DIGITIMES*, November 14, 2011, http://www.digitimes.com/news/a20111114PD209.html.

4   Andy Grove, "How America Can Create Jobs," *Bloomberg Businessweek*, July 1, 2010.

5   Sophia Cheng, "The Deadly Labor Behind Our Phones, Laptops and Consumer Gadgets", *Colorlines*, September 1, 2011, http://colorlines.com/archives/2011/09/the_deadly_labor_of_consumer_electronics.html.

6   Peter Navarro, *The Coming China Wars: Where They Will Be Fought, And How They Can Be Won* (FT Press, 2006), p.89.

7   Joseph Kahn and Jim Yardley, *"As China Roars, Pollution Reaches Deadly Extremes,"* *The New York Times*, August 26, 2007.

8   *The Anti-Apartheid Movement: A 40-Year Perspective* (South Africa House: 1999).

9   http://www.newbalance.com/usa/#/made-in-usa.

10 Peter Whoriskey, "New Balance Stuggles as Last Major Athletic Shoe Brand Still Manufacturing In U.S.," *The Washington Post*, July 28, 2011.

11 http://www.newbalance.com/usa/#/made-in-usa.

12 Dana Frank, *Buy American: The Untold Story of Economic Nationalism* (Boston: Beacon Press, 1999), p. 211.

Chapter 8: Making Your Dollar Count

1   "U.S. Trade in Goods and Services – Balance of Payments (BOP) Basis 1960 Thru 2010, *U.S. Census Bureau*, Historical Series, June 2011, http://www.census.gov/foreign-trade/statistics/historical/gands.txt.

2   Ha-Joon Chang, *23 Things They Don't Tell You About Capitalism*, p. 237.

3   Thomas Black, "More Car Jobs Shift to Mexico," *Bloomberg Businessweek*, June 24, 2010.

4   This calculation is based on going from a .25 ratio to 1.0 (in one year) .75 x $4,000 = $3,000. 230 million x $3,000 = $690 billion, more than our present trade deficit. This takes into account the fact that we are unlikely to buy only 100% American goods and 0% foreign goods, and includes the trade ratio to illustrate this. It is of course a simplification—what is important is that individual shifts in spending add up.

4   Peter Coy, "The Case For Making It in the USA," *Bloomberg Businessweek*, May 5, 2011.

6   Ibid.

7   Nick Leiber, "Made in USA Gives Small Business an Edge," *Bloomberg Businessweek*, March 24, 2011.

8   Ibid.

9   Chris Isidore, "Made in USA: Overseas Jobs Come Home," *CNNMoney*, June 17, 2011, http://money.cnn.com/2011/06/17/news/economy/made_in_usa/index.htm.

10 Melissa Eversley, "Made in USA Store to Open Near Buffalo," *USA Today*, May 20, 2010.

11 "Global 500: Our Annual Ranking of the World's Largest Corporations," *Fortune*, 2011.

12 Miguel Bustillo and Ann Zimmerman, "Wal-Mart Sparks War Among Big Toy Sellers," *The Wall Street Journal*, October 9, 2008.

13 Jiang Jingjing, "Wal-Mart's China Inventory to Hit US $18b This Year," *China Daily*, November 29th, 2004.

Consumer Travelogue Source Material

Information for all profiles came from the following:

National Geographic Atlas of the World, Eight Edition (National Geographic, 2004)

BBC News Country Profiles at http://news.bbc.co.uk/2/hi/country_profiles/default.stm.

CIA World Factbook 2011

Peter Stalker: Oxford Guide to the Countries in the World (Oxford University Press: 2010)

Yale University's "2010 Environmental Performance Index"

Freedom House: "Freedom in the World 2011"

Transparency International: "2010 World Corruption Index"

United States Department of Commerce's Office of Travel and Tourism Industries: "2009 United States Resident Travel Abroad"

2011 List of Sourcing Countries, The Gap Social Responsibility, http://www.gapinc.com/content/csr/html/topnavtoolbar/faq.html

Reebok Global Supplier List: http://www.reebok.com/Static/global/initiatives/rights/textonly/business/suppliers.html

"Active Factories," Nike, http://www.nikebiz.com/responsibility/documents/factory_disclosure_list.pdf

"Levi Strauss & Co. Factory List," http://www.levistrauss.com/sites/default/files/librarydocument/2011/9/lsco-factory-list-may-2011a.pdf

Adidas Group Global Supplier Factory List: http://www.adidas-group.com/en/sustainability/suppliers_and_workers/default.aspx

Notes for Travelogue

Argentina:

1 "Wine production," Food and Agriculture Organization, 2011.

Australia:

2 The Conference Board of Canada, "Environment : Organic Farming", October 2008, http://www.conferenceboard.ca/hcp/details/environment/area-under-organic-farming.aspx.

3 Barry Fitzgerald, "Australia Still No. 2 Gold Producer," The Sydney Morning Herald, February 28th, 2011.

Bangladesh:

4 "Levi Strauss & Co. Factory List," http://www.levistrauss.com/sites/default/files/librarydocument/2011/9/lsco-factory-list-may-2011a.pdf.

5 Muhammad Azizul Islam, Social and Environmental Reporting Practices of Organisations Operating in, or Sourcing Products from, a Developing Country: Evidence from Bangladesh, RMIT University, 2009, p. 4. Accessible at : http://adt.lib.rmit.edu.au/adt/uploads/approved/adt-VIT20090821.145037/public/02WHOLE.pdf.

Belgium:

6 "Facilities" at media.ford.com, http://media.ford.com/plants.cfm?region=NA.

7 Leo Cendrowicz, "Belgian Waffling: Who Needs Government, Anyway," Time, February 21, 2011.

Brazil:

8 "U.S. Tops Brazil as Top Ethanol Producer of 2010," Daily Energy Report, http://www.dailyenergyreport.com/2011/02/united-states-tops-brazil-as-top-ethanol-producer-of-2010/.

Canada:

9 "U.S. Export Fact Sheet," U.S. Department of Commerce International Trade Administration, April 2010, http://2001-2009.commerce.gov/s/groups/public/@doc/@os/@opa/documents/content/prod01_009101.pdf.

10 "Travel Between Canada and Other Countries," Statistics Canada, November 2010, http://www.statcan.gc.ca/daily-quotidien/110119/dq110119c-eng.htm.

Chile:

11 2009 Corporate Responsibility Report", Goodyear, available at http://www.goodyear.com/corporate/about/responsibility/.

China:

12 Jiang Jingjing, "Wal-Mart's China Inventory to Hit US $18b This Year," *China Daily*, November 29, 2004.

13 Lisa Friedman, "China Leads Major Countries with $34.6 Billion Invested in Clean Technology," *The New York Times*, March 25, 2010.

Costa Rica:

14 "Summary of Production and R&D Facilities,", Bridgestone Tires, http://www.bridgestone.com/corporate/locations/index.html.

Denmark:

15 Arthur Max, "China and Denmark Lead the Way in Clean Technology," *news.com.au*, May 8, 2011.

Dominican Republic:

16 "Dominican Republic: World Leader in Organic Banana Exports," *Freshplaza.com*, August 2011, http://www.freshplaza.com/news_detail.asp?id=84838.

17 "2011 Opening Day MLB Rosters Feature 234 Foreign-Born Players," *Major League Baseball*, April 1, 2011.

Finland:

18 "Nuclear Power in Finland," *World Nuclear Association*, June 2011, http://world-nuclear.org/info/inf76.html.

Guatemala:

19 "Coffees of Guatemala," http://www.rombouts.com/uk/univers/coffee-producing-countries/.

20 Barbara Schieber, "Guatemala the World's Biggest Producer of Cardamom," *Guatemala Times*, December 18, 2008.

Ireland:

21 "In Ireland Since 1989," *Intel*, http://www.intel.com/corporate/europe/emea/irl/intel/about.htm.

22 "Manufacturing Sites", Hasbro, http://www.hasbro.com/corporate/corporate-social-responsibility/global-manufacturing-ethics-sites.cfm.

23 Kevin Hoffman, "How the Celtic Tiger Became the World's Software Export Champ," *Spiegel Online International*, March 3, 2006, http://www.spiegel.de/international/spiegel/0,1518,348682,00.html.

24 "Tourism and Travel," *Central Statistics Office Ireland*, http://www.cso.ie/statistics/vistoirenumoseasvisits.htm.

Israel:

25 Eli Stutz, "Israel, World Leader in Recycled Water," *IsraelNationalNews.com*, May 24, 2010.

Italy:

26 "Italy World Leader for Organic Wine Production," *Italy Magazine*, June 17, 2008.

27 Tracy Wilkinson, "Italy Leads World as Top Producer of Kiwis," *The Seattle Times*, May 26, 2008.

Mexico:

28 Ryan Dube, "Mexico Passes Peru as World's Top Silver Producer," *Market Watch*, September 2, 2011.

Netherlands:

29 "The Netherlands Is the World's Largest Exporter of Fresh Vegetables," *Dutch Daily News*, May 19, 2010, http://www.dutchdailynews.com/the-netherlands-is-world%E2%80%99s-largest-exporter-of-fresh-vegetables/.

New Zealand:

30 Tracy Withers, "New Zealand Tourism Overtakes Dairy As Largest Export Industry," *Bloomberg,* October 26, 2010.

Nigeria:

31 "Nigeria Surpasses Hollywood as World's Second Largest Film Producer – UN", *UN News Centre,* May 5, 2009, http://www.un.org/apps/news/story.asp?NewsID=30707.

Pakistan:

32 "Levi Strauss & Co. Factory List," http://www.levistrauss.com/sites/default/files/librarydocument/2011/9/lsco-factory-list-may-2011a.pdf.

33 "Soccer Balls", *The United States Department of Labor, Bureau of International Labor Affairs,* http://www.dol.gov/ilab/media/reports/iclp/sweat4/soccer.htm.

Peru:

34 "2009 Corporate Responsibility Report", Goodyear, available at http://www.goodyear.com/corporate/about/responsibility/.

Portugal:

35 J.L. Calheiros E Meneses, "The Cork Industry in Portugal," accessed at http://www.uwec.edu/geography/ivogeler/travel/portugal/cork-article2.htm.

36 Elizabeth Rosenthal, "Portugal Makes Itself a Clean-Energy Makeover", *The New York Times,* August 9th, 2010.

Switzerland:

37 "Industries/Service – Trade and Investment," *The Trade Office of Swiss Industries,* http://www.swiss.org.tw/trade/industries.htm.

Thailand:

38 Nilaratna Xuto, "Thailand: Conciliating a Dispute on Tuna Exports to the EC," *World Trade Organization,* Managing the Challenges of WTO Participation, Case Study 40, http://www.wto.org/english/res_e/booksp_e/casestudies_e/case40_e.htm.

39 Sinfah Tunsarawuth, "Thai Rubber Exports in 2011 Seen to Double in Value on Soaring World Price," *People's Daily Online,* February 25, 2011.

Venezuela:

40 "Oil Leak: Could One of the World's Top Petroleum Producers Really Go Bankrupt?", *The Economist,* February 24, 2011.

41 Benoit Faucon, "Venezuela's Oil Reserves Top Saudi Arabia's, OPEC Says," *The Wall Street Journal,* July 18, 2011.

Vietnam:

42 "Vietnam Takes China's Place as Top Nike Producer," *Want China Times,* July 1, 2011, http://www.wantchinatimes.com/news-subclass-cnt.aspx?id=20110701000011&cid=1102&MainCatID=11.

ABOUT THE AUTHOR

Alan Uke (pronounced U-K) is a San Diego businessman, entrepreneur, and community leader.

He still runs his company, Underwater Kinetics, which he started 41 years ago during his sophomore year at the University of California at San Diego. He holds over 40 patents and his SCUBA diving and industrial lighting products are now exported to over 60 countries. Mr. Uke has won the Entrepreneur of the Year Award for Consumer Products from Entrepreneur of the Year Institute. He was also a member of the Young Presidents' Organization (YPO) and is presently a member of the World Presidents' Organization (WPO).

Mr. Uke has also been involved at the highest levels of civic and community service boards. His past experience includes holding the position of Fundraising Chair for the Desert Pacific Chapter of Boy Scouts of America, Vice Chair of St. Vincent De Paul Village in Charge of the Self-Help and Resource Exchange (SHARE), President of the San Diego Taxpayers Educational Foundation, President of North County Council on Aging, and board member of the San Diego County Area on Aging Advisory Council. He was awarded the Dr. Lutz Award for lifetime service to the senior community. In November of 2004 Alan was presented with the 2004 Patriot of the Year by the Desert Pacific Council Chapter of Boy Scouts of America.

He conceived of and founded the San Diego Aircraft Carrier Museum. Mr. Uke now serves as its Founder and President Emeritus. The group successfully acquired the USS *Midway* and opened it as a public museum in June of 2004.

Alan Uke was born in Santa Monica, California. Mr. Uke has lived in San Diego County since 1970 and has three children. He and his wife Amie live in Del Mar.

For further information about this book, and more information related to the consumer movement to pass new product country of origin labeling laws, please visit our website at:

www.BuyingAmericaBack.org

☆ PERSONAL PLEDGE ☆

I, _____ , pledge to
make conscious spending choices to support &
create American jobs by committing to purchase
American-made products or products from the
most equal trade partners whenever possible.

_____
(signature)

_____
(date)

If each American spent as little as an additional $1 a
day for American-made products we would save over 1
million American jobs. Spending an additional $5 a day
would save 5 million jobs annually. Spending $10 more
a day would save 10 million jobs.

JOIN THE MOVEMENT, SPREAD THE WORD, AND GET CONNECTED!

Sign the pledge and register your support at
www.BuyingAmericaBack.org